*The Long Shadow of Vatican II*

*October 1 2013*

*With respect and gratitude for your March 5th support!*

# The Long Shadow of
# Vatican II

*Living Faith and Negotiating Authority
since the Second Vatican Council*

EDITED BY Lucas Van Rompay, Sam Miglarese,
and David Morgan

*The University of North Carolina Press   Chapel Hill*

*Publication of this book was assisted by a grant from the Duke University Department of Religious Studies and three of its endowments: the John-Kelly C. Warren Roman Catholic Studies Endowment Fund, the Evelyn and Valfrid Palmer Roman Catholic Studies Endowment Fund, and the Dennis and Rita Meyer Endowment Fund.*

Set in Miller by codeMantra, Inc.
Manufactured in the United States of America
The paper in this book meets the guidelines for permanence and durability of the Committee on Production Guidelines for Book Longevity of the Council on Library Resources. The University of North Carolina Press has been a member of the Green Press Initiative since 2003.

Cover illustration: Wayside cross near Marieville, Quebec, Canada, erected in 2011. Used by permission of the photographer, Monique Bellemare (www.patrimoineduquebec.com).

Library of Congress Cataloging-in-Publication Data
The long shadow of Vatican II : authority, faith, and church since the
Second Vatican Council (1962–1965) / edited by Lucas Van Rompay,
Sam Miglarese, and David Morgan. — 1 [edition].
    pages cm
Includes bibliographical references and index.
ISBN 978-1-4696-2529-4 (pbk : alk. paper) —
ISBN 978-1-4696-2530-0 (ebook : alk. paper)
1. Vatican Council (2nd : 1962–1965 : Basilica di San Pietro in Vaticano) 2. Catholic Church—United States—History—21st century. I. Rompay, Lucas van, joint editor.
BX8301962 .L58 2015
262'.52—dc23
2015002755

THIS BOOK WAS DIGITALLY PRINTED.

*Contents*

# Figures

# Acknowledgments

It is a pleasant task to express our thanks to Duke University's Department of Religious Studies. The department first supported our initiative to commemorate the fiftieth anniversary of the opening of the Second Vatican Council with a lecture series in the fall of 2012. This lecture series subsequently developed and expanded into the present publication. The department allowed us to use the resources of the Dennis and Rita Meyer Endowment Fund, the Evelyn and Valfrid Palmer Roman Catholic Studies Endowment Fund, and the John-Kelly C. Warren Roman Catholic Studies Endowment Fund. In addition to the organization of the lecture series, we employed these resources to defray the costs of the publication of this volume.

For the preparation of the volume and the work on the illustrations we greatly benefited from the editorial assistance of Jamie Brummit, a graduate student in Duke University's Graduate Program in Religion.

We are grateful that our volume was accepted for publication by the University of North Carolina Press. The skillful guidance of the Press's editorial staff made the process of preparation and publication smooth and pleasant, and allowed us to fully benefit from the constructive comments of the two external readers.

Lucas Van Rompay, Sam Miglarese, and David Morgan

*The Long Shadow of Vatican II*

# INTRODUCTION

*Lucas Van Rompay, Sam Miglarese, and David Morgan*


Recognized as the twenty-first Ecumenical Council in the history of the Roman Catholic Church, the Second Vatican Council opened its doors in October 1962. The Council convened nearly one hundred years after the much shorter First Vatican Council (1869–70) and more than four hundred years after the Council of Trent (1545–63). Prior to 1962, therefore, the Catholic Church had never deployed its broadest and most representative conciliar structure in its struggle with modernity. Both for its massive and truly global character and as the Church's first attempt at taking a more positive stance on modernity, the Council ranks among the most significant religious events of the twentieth century.

Compelled by an imperative that resulted from popular sentiment, lived experience, and both internal and external pressures to reform, Pope John XXIII convened the Second Vatican Council to address many of the urgent issues that preoccupied twentieth-century Catholic laypeople and clergy. The liturgical movement, the revival of biblical and patristic studies, and heightened ecumenical sensitivity range among the dramatic influences that formed the background to the Council's deliberations and decisions.

While steering a prudent middle course between tradition and innovation, between continuity and change, the Council Fathers made a number of momentous decisions that forever changed the way of thinking, worshiping, and acting of the Catholic community. Too rash for some and too timid for others, many of the reforms made or considered by the Council initiated a dynamic process of questioning, renewal, and transformation that today—more than fifty years later—has by no means subsided.

This volume commemorates the fiftieth anniversary of the closing of the Second Vatican Council. In providing a select history of Vatican II, it illuminates and assesses crucial aspects of the Council, including its reception and interpretation in twenty-first-century North America. Leo D. Lefebure discusses the Council and its effects on interreligious relations, Leslie W. Tentler examines the Council's American reception and

1

legacy, and Catherine E. Clifford explores the exercise of ecclesial author-ity. Jill Peterfeso looks into the legacy of women's empowerment within the Church, and Hillary Kaell examines how the Council affected public and private devotions. On a broader level, the volume as a whole illumi-nates the effects of Vatican II on the lived religion of everyday Catholics.

The process of decision making and the question of "what happened" at the Council—to echo the title of the authoritative 2008 book by John W. O'Malley—receive appropriate attention in each of the essays. But much more important in the authors' approaches is the impact that the Council and its decisions had on the Church and its faithful in the fol-lowing decades. It is the "long shadow" of the Council, extending well into the twenty-first century, that serves as the prism through which the present volume views the Council. While the sixteen documents of the Council at first sight seem to cohere neatly, with the "spirit" of the Coun-cil serving as a powerful unifying factor, a closer analysis of the texts reveals some of the tensions underlying the Council discussions—often reflecting different views of the Church or the modern world. Such ten-sions make us aware that the Council documents are not always as final and as closed as they first appear and may in fact invite ongoing reflec-tions and evolving interpretations. The changing world of the interpreter also contributes to what may be seen as an ongoing process of dynamic interaction between the Council and subsequent generations of observ-ers and receivers. Perceptions of the Church and its place in the modern world have rapidly changed throughout the years, and the Council's initial *aggiornamento* (a bringing up to date) needs to be retuned and reevaluated for our postmodern world. It is the Council, its reception, and its reinterpretation in the twenty-first century that constitute the overall theme of this volume.

The volume opens with an essay on Catholic interreligious relations by Leo D. Lefebure: "Is There Reason for Hope? The Second Vatican Council and Catholic Interreligious Relations." This essay offers much more than a discussion of the ways in which the Catholic Church views the non-Christian world. It rather brings us to the heart of Catholic self-reflection and self-definition in the present. Two Declarations, on non-Christian religions (*Nostra Aetate*) and on religious liberty (*Digni-tatis Humanae*)—the latter honoring human conscience as one's ulti-mate moral guide—have given the faithful a perspective on themselves and on other religions that is still developing today. The mind-set at the core of these two texts differs dramatically from the one prevailing in the mid-twentieth century.

Leslie Woodcock Tentler's essay, "The American Reception and Legacy of the Second Vatican Council," focuses on the incumbency of the influential archbishop of Detroit, John Francis Dearden (archbishop from 1958 to 1980, made a cardinal in 1969). While reviewing the many changes in Catholic life—including the relationship between the Church hierarchy and the laity, the role of women in society, and the thorny issues of sexuality and procreation—the essay shows how the Church leadership found itself caught up in larger trends in American society during the tumultuous sixties that lay beyond its control. The essay also shows how different groups used and interpreted the decisions of the Council in different ways for different purposes.

In Catherine E. Clifford's essay, "The Exercise of Ecclesial Authority in Light of Vatican II," the processes and structures of decision making and the exercise of authority itself come under examination. While in several of the Council documents the Church expressed its commitment to a decidedly new approach to authority, thus raising high expectations on the part of an educated clergy and a responsible laity, the implementation of real changes subsequently met with many challenges. As outlined in Clifford's work, the past fifty years have shown a difficult learning process, for both the Church and its faithful, as well as a mixed legacy.

The Council did not discuss the question of women's access to the ministerial priesthood—much to the disappointment of some, mostly European, women who thought the time ripe for such consideration. Vatican II tacitly assumed the official position of the Catholic Church on this matter, consisting of a total rejection of the idea of women's eligibility to ordination, and this position was reaffirmed by the Sacred Congregation for the Doctrine of the Faith in its 1976 declaration, On the Question of Admission of Women to the Ministerial Priesthood (*Inter Insigniores*). It was argued that "the priestly office cannot become the goal of social advancement" and that "no merely human progress of society or of the individual can of itself give access to it: it is of another order." This position has been repeated time and again, under successive popes, to the present day.

Such a position was obviously bound to provoke reactions and discussion—during Vatican II, with the release of *Inter Insigniores*, and until today. Focusing on the twenty-first-century movement of Roman Catholic Womenpriests, Jill Peterfeso in her essay, "Vatican II and the History of Interpretation: The Case of Roman Catholic Womenpriests," examines the arguments used by women who refused to be silenced. These women found some of their arguments in the Council documents themselves, in particular in the Constitution on the Church (*Lumen*

*Gentium*) and on the Church in the Modern World (*Gaudium et Spes*), which spoke in favor of the empowerment of laypeople and against all sorts of discrimination. This essay, therefore, returns us to the crucial issue of interpretation, to be understood as a dynamic process in which both the multilayered texts and the—never disengaged—readers operate as the driving forces and meaning-creating authorities.

Hillary Kaell's essay, "Quebec's Wayside Crosses and the Creation of Contemporary Devotionalism," takes us to a different level of the Council's reception. What effect did the Council's promotion and reform of the liturgy, the public worship of the Church—as laid out in the Constitution on the Sacred Liturgy (*Sacrosanctum Concilium*)—have on Christians' popular devotions? It is generally assumed that the Council did not leave much room for public devotion outside the reformed and newly endorsed patterns of the Catholic liturgy. Kaell's essay, however, dealing with the three thousand crosses that still decorate the landscape in the Canadian province of Quebec, shows a much more complex picture than the gradual disappearance of devotional life. What we are witnessing here is in fact not the demise, but rather the redefinition of public devotion. The devotionalism associated with Quebec's wayside crosses creatively makes use of some of the key notions of the Council, which are adjusted in a rather pragmatic way to the daily experiences of traditional Catholics in the late twentieth and early twenty-first century.

A recurrent theme throughout the volume is the tension that has always existed within the Catholic Church between what its hierarchy considers important to maintain and what its laity find moving and powerful in daily life. The two aspects do not always align. When we think of the significance of Vatican II regarding this tension, we must recognize the additional strain between reformers within the Church and those who resist significant change in the belief that maintaining tradition is essential. So the three forces continue to interact and struggle over the "true" meaning of the Council and its legacy. Reformers inspired by John XXIII want to see change within the Catholic tradition as a positive development and consequence of the Second Vatican Council. Traditionalists regard the emphasis on the Council as an agent of change as inaccurate. And the laity sometimes regret the loss of traditional devotional practices in the wave of liturgical reform and the shift away from a number of cherished practices such as the Stations of the Cross, a number of saints' cults, and the so-called Tridentine mass.

The lay dimension of Catholic life since Vatican II has taken a number of directions. While it is true that the Christo-centric character of the Council diminished the emphasis traditionally placed on saints, the Church has maintained a strong commitment to lay piety, which was clearly mandated in the Council's documents. While St. Patrick has tended to pass from beloved saint to civic holiday festival in the United States, Marian piety has flourished, many traditional devotions such as the Sacred Heart of Jesus have rebounded, and the interest in the so-called Tridentine Mass increased. The Council has shaped Catholicism as lived religion in at least two broad ways. On the one hand, the recognition of lay-centered and lay-driven movements within the parish and beyond has led to expanded efforts, sometimes even beyond the purview of what the hierarchy would sanction, or at least would prefer not to see take hold. Women's movements of various kinds, such as the move toward female ordination, though by no means promoted by the Council, might nevertheless be said to draw some support from the legacy of the Council's recognition of the importance of lay engagement. On the other hand, conservative initiatives have partially arisen as ways of appropriating or curbing the interpretation of the Council as a force for reform.

Considering the long shadow of the Second Vatican Council and the search for the supposedly true meaning of the Council in our day, one is unavoidably confronted with the radically different historical contexts of the Council itself, on the one hand, and of its later reception, on the other. The Council was convened at a time when the new hopes and the optimism of post–World War II reconstruction rapidly turned into the fears and anxieties inspired by the realities of the new political global landscape, determined by the Cold War and the process of decolonization. The texts and legacy of the Council cannot be stripped of this specific historical context, but they do need to be reread and reinterpreted in the light of the new paradigms of our age. This may come with the painful awareness that in our postcolonial and postmodern world, many of the certainties of the past are gone and that our quest for understanding may be a "search for instabilities" (*recherche des instabilités*), to quote a phrase from Jean-François Lyotard's 1979 detailed analysis of knowledge in the postmodern era.

The five essays of this volume, then, offer windows through which to view the different and complementary responses to the Council during the past fifty years. While we are dealing with the Catholic Church as a global institution with worldwide ramifications, much of the reception history laid out in this volume focuses on the United States and Canada. The essays deliberately provide both insider and outsider perspectives to evaluate the legacy of one of the Council's main goals: to reassert the role of "the Church in the modern world." In the twenty-first century, interpreting and evaluating the role of the Church in the modern world has proven an even more complex task than the Council Fathers could have fathomed fifty years ago.

All the essays included in this volume were first written in 2012, at a time when much of the discussion on the legacy of the Council was dominated, and had been dominated for some time, by the opposing views of continuity versus discontinuity, traditionalism versus reform, leading in some areas to a stalemate. That the two most recent popes, John Paul II (1978–2005) and Benedict XVI (2005–13), showed hesitation in their dealings with the Council and occasionally sent out mixed messages left the faithful and the clergy wondering whether the process of reform initiated by the Council had stalled and where the Church was heading. In the early spring of 2013 no one could have predicted that with the surprising resignation of Pope Benedict XVI and the subsequent election of the Argentinian Jesuit, Jorge Mario Cardinal Bergoglio, the new Pope Francis, a new chapter in our thinking about the Council would be inaugurated. The charismatic and untraditional new pope immediately raised the hope and the expectation that he, and with him the Roman Catholic Church, would be able to overcome division and weakness and to inject new energy and confidence into the process of necessary reform. At the present moment—only one year into the tenure of the new pope—it is too early to measure or evaluate any kind of change that has taken place. But the atmosphere of open and honest dialogue that has characterized Pope Francis's first year, as well as some of his concrete actions, statements, and publications, have definitely put things in a new light. As a result, some of the essays in our volume required an update or at least a new final thought. In fact, Pope Francis's first apostolic exhortation, *Evangelii Gaudium* (The Joy of the Gospel), issued in November 2013, has changed the tone of the Catholic Church's interaction with other religions, as Lefebure duly notes in his essay on interreligious dialogue. As for the exercise of ecclesial authority, Clifford highlights some topics in the same exhortation that may indicate, on the part of the new pontiff, a renewed effort and willingness to implement some of the necessary changes recommended by the Second Vatican Council.

While the theme of joy in the title of the new pope's first apostolic exhortation echoes the title of Pope John's XXIII 1962 opening address to the Council, *Gaudet Mater Ecclesia* (Mother Church Rejoices), as pointed out by Lefebure, it is too early to tell how far the similarity between Pope John XXIII and Pope Francis will go and whether the latter will be as much committed as the former to "scrutinizing the signs of the times" (*Gaudium et Spes*, 4). But Pope Francis's new style of openness has added a novel perspective to many of the issues dealt with in this volume. This moment of transition and expectation gives to the essays of the present work an additional layer of significance, one waiting to be fully disclosed in the future.

## 1

## IS THERE REASON FOR HOPE?

The Second Vatican Council and Catholic Interreligious Relations

*Leo D. Lefebure*

Prelude

On June 13, 1960, two aging men, both octogenarians, meet in the Vatican: Jules Isaac is a French Jewish historian who has lost many of his family, including his wife and his daughter, in the Shoah and who has studied the history of Catholic attitudes toward Jews and Judaism; he has requested an audience with Pope John XXIII, who as a wartime papal diplomat in Istanbul had helped Jews in southeastern Europe to obtain transit visas to escape the Nazis and who recently as pope has called for a second ecumenical council to convene in the Vatican.[1] Isaac expresses the tremendous hopes of the Jewish people regarding Pope John: "If we expect still more, what is responsible for that, if not the great 'goodness of the Pope'?"[2] Isaac requests that the upcoming ecumenical council correct the false and unjust statements about Israel and the Jewish people in traditional Catholic teaching. In particular, he mentions the traditional Catholic view that God punished the Jews for the crucifixion of Jesus by scattering them among the nations. The Jewish historian knows Catholic teaching quite well; to support his case, he cites the Roman Catechism issued in 1566 after the Council of Trent, which taught that Jesus died for the sins of all humans. Isaac proposes that this official teaching of the Catholic Church contradicts the widespread claim that Jews are uniquely guilty of deicide, the attempted murder of God. At the end of the audience, Isaac poses the poignant question of whether there is reason to hope. Pope John replies: "You have reason for more than hope."[3]

Neither Jules Isaac nor Pope John XXIII would live until October 1965 to see the promulgation of the Declaration on the Church's Relation to Non-Christian Religions, often known by its opening Latin words as *Nostra Aetate*; but they are arguably the two most important individuals setting in motion the process that led to this document. Both men know that behind

Jules Isaac (1877–1963), the author of *The Teaching of Contempt: Christian Roots of Anti-Semitism* (L'enseignement du mépris, 1962). Isaac's meeting with Pope John XXIII in June 1960 helped shape Jewish-Catholic relations during and after the Council. From André Kaspi, *Jules Isaac ou la passion de la vérité* (Paris: Plon, 2002), 184. (Courtesy of André Kaspi)

their encounter stretch centuries of Catholic animosity toward Jews, shaped by a hostile reading of the Bible.[4] Isaac is convinced that Catholic-Jewish relations have been marred by false beliefs and perceptions on the part of Catholics; he hopes that a more accurate reading of the sources of the Catholic tradition can correct these errors and improve this relationship. Thus he prods Pope John and other Catholics to review their Bible and tradition with a more benign attitude toward Jews and Judaism.[5]

The horrors of the Shoah during World War II had dramatically changed the context of Catholic relations with Jews, and Isaac was by no means alone in his concerns. Even though Nazism was profoundly anti-Christian, by 1960 many Catholics had come to view the long history of Catholic animosity toward Jews as a tragic, sinful legacy that required rejection.[6] In 1960, both the Pontifical Biblical Institute in Rome and the Institute of Judaeo-Christian Studies of Seton Hall University in New Jersey sent petitions to the Central Preparatory Commission requesting that the upcoming ecumenical council condemn anti-Semitism and improve the Catholic Church's relations to the Jewish people. Meanwhile, an international working group of priests and laypersons met in Apeldoorn, the Netherlands, in August 1960 and sent a detailed memorandum calling for a conciliar statement on the Catholic Church's relationship to the Jewish people.[7]

A number of Catholics who came from a Jewish background played a pivotal role in transforming Catholic attitudes toward Jews and in preparing for the Second Vatican Council. Johannes M. Oesterreicher and Annie Kraus, both originally Jews who became Catholics, pioneered efforts against Catholic anti-Jewish attitudes in the years before the Council opened. Gregory Baum and Bruno Hussar, also converts to Catholicism from Jewish backgrounds, proved instrumental as well. But even earlier, since the 1840s, some Catholic converts, most of whom originally came from Jewish backgrounds, had labored against Catholic anti-Jewish attitudes. John Connelly asserts: *"Without converts the Catholic Church would not have found a new language to speak to the Jews after the Holocaust.* As such, the story of *Nostra Aetate* is an object lesson on the sources but also the limits of solidarity."[8]

In fact, the problem was far broader than relations with Jews alone. The Catholic Church in 1960 inherited a history of conflicted and often violent relationships with virtually every other religious tradition on this planet. One of the most serious obstacles to interreligious relations was the long-standing position that the Catholic Church denied any right to religious liberty for non-Catholics, but insisted on religious liberty for Catholics when they were threatened. In his 1832 encyclical *Mirari Vos*, Pope Gregory XVI set the tone for Catholic interreligious attitudes through his condemnation of "indifferentism": "This perverse opinion is spread on all sides by the fraud of the wicked who claim that *it is possible to obtain the eternal salvation of the soul by the profession of any kind of religion, as long as morality is maintained.*"[9] In accord with this perspective, Pope Gregory condemned the notion of liberty of conscience in religion: "This shameful font of indifferentism gives rise to that absurd and erroneous proposition which claims that **liberty of conscience** must be maintained for everyone" [bold in online version].[10] In 1960, this remained the teaching of the Catholic Church. The American Jesuit theologian John Courtney Murray had already advocated religious freedom, but the Holy See had ordered him to be silent on the issue.[11]

Catholic attitudes toward all other religions had historically been overwhelmingly hostile. Catholics traditionally viewed Muslims (who were named "Saracens" in official church statements)[12] as forerunners and allies of the Antichrist and as associates of the Son of Destruction of 2 Thessalonians 2:3.[13] Catholics often viewed Hindus and Buddhists as idolaters who bowed down before the graven images condemned in the Bible.[14] There were, to be sure, Catholics who proposed more generous, respectful interpretations of other religions.[15] In the nineteenth century, some Catholics believed that there had been a primordial revelation to the first humans and that this had left positive traces in various religious traditions.[16] When the World Parliament of Religions was held at the Columbian Exposition in Chicago in 1893, the leading American Catholic churchman of the day, James Cardinal Gibbons of Baltimore, participated and supported cordial interreligious relations, as did Chicago's Archbishop Patrick Feehan.[17] Yet the Apostolic Delegate in Washington, D.C., Archbishop Francesco Satolli, wrote a negative report on the Parliament of Religions to Rome, and Pope Leo XIII forbade Catholic participation in any future interreligious assemblies.[18] In the early and middle twentieth century, a number of Catholics appreciatively explored other religions and developed friendly interreligious relationships.[19] But in 1960, these more respectful and friendly voices had relatively little influence on the official Catholic magisterium. No Catholic ecumenical council in history had ever issued a positive statement about other religions.

After the audience with Jules Isaac, Pope John XXIII conferred with the Jesuit scripture scholar Augustin Cardinal Bea and at his recommendation directed the newly formed Secretariat for Promoting Christian Unity to develop a reflection on "the Jewish question" as part of the preparations for the Council.[20] As soon as the news spread that the upcoming ecumenical council would consider making a statement on the relation of the Catholic Church to the Jewish people, intense and widespread controversy began; Arab governments were especially concerned that such a declaration would open the way for Catholic relations with the State of Israel.[21] In response, both on the floor of the Second Vatican Council and outside, Cardinal Bea repeatedly insisted that the developing statement on relations with the Jewish people was a purely religious and theological document with no political ramifications.[22] Yet many in the Middle East did not recognize any such distinction.

The Second Vatican Council was by far the most international ecumenical council in the history of the Catholic Church, with 2,600 delegates coming from 134 countries throughout the world. As the discussions developed, bishops from around the world pointed out that there were other religions than Judaism and urged the inclusion of other religious traditions in the prospective statement. Thus what began as a statement on "the Jewish question" attached to the schema on Christian ecumenism developed into a broader, independent declaration on the relation of the Catholic Church to all other religions.

Both before and during the Council, the discussions of a possible statement regarding other religions proved long, difficult, and controversial.[23] At least three groups raised questions about the wisdom of a statement on other religions: (1) conservative Catholics such as Archbishop Marcel Lefebvre, who rejected religious liberty and insisted that both Scripture and Catholic tradition had already judged the Jewish people and that no conciliar statement could change established Church teaching;[24] (2) Arab governments, who lobbied strenuously against any statement that would exonerate the Jews from responsibility for the death of Jesus or recognize the legitimacy of the Jewish state; and (3) Christians from the Middle East who expressed a number of concerns from a variety of viewpoints. Jewish observers watched carefully as the discussions proceeded through various stages. When one of the drafts of the projected statement expressed hope for the eventual union of the Jewish people and the Catholic Church, Abraham Joshua Heschel, the leading Jewish theologian in the United States at that time, came to Rome and met with Pope Paul VI and other Catholic leaders; he expressed the apprehensions of the Jewish community that this statement implied the elimination of the Jewish people through conversion. It did not appear in the final declaration.

While the number of Christian representatives from the Middle East in the Second Vatican Council remained relatively small, their voices carried immense influence on this topic. On August 31, 1962, just before the Council opened, the Holy Synod of the Melkite Greek Catholic Church met in Aïn-Traz, Lebanon, and issued a manifesto that argued that the biblical promises of land to the Jewish people had long since been fulfilled in biblical times and could not be invoked to support Jewish conquest and appropriation of land in the present. The synod took no position on the modern State of Israel, but it insisted on justice for the Arabs of Palestine and proposed to the coming Council: "The Church must therefore consider the subject of Judaism in a spiritual-religious context. The council ought not to intervene in civil and political issues."[25]

Pope Paul VI meeting with the American Jewish leader Abraham Joshua Heschel (1971). Heschel was the principal American Jewish interlocutor of Cardinal Bea during the Council and remained involved in Jewish-Catholic dialogue well after the Council. Courtesy of David M. Rubenstein Rare Book and Manuscript Library, Duke University. (© Osservatore Romano)

## The Second Vatican Council

On October 11, 1962, Pope John delivered the opening speech of the Second Vatican Council, *Gaudet Mater Ecclesia* (Mother Church Rejoices); in it he decried "those prophets of gloom who are forecasting disaster as though the end of the world were at hand."[26] The Cuban missile crisis was first developing at this time, and just a week later, Pope John played a significant role in mediating between the Soviet premier, Nikita Khrushchev, and the U.S. president, John Kennedy. Amid serious threats, Pope John rejected the warnings of the "prophets of gloom" and presented a moving vision of joy and hope. Even though he died in 1963, before any conciliar statements on other religions were issued, his spirit and especially his hope for humans to form one community pervade the conciliar documents.

While the central statement of the Second Vatican Council on the Catholic Church's relation to other religions is found in *Nostra Aetate*, other documents of the Council played a vital role in changing Catholic interreligious relationships, including most importantly the four constitutions *Sacrosanctum Concilium* (the Dogmatic Constitution on the Sacred Liturgy), *Lumen Gentium* (the Dogmatic Constitution on the Church), *Dei Verbum* (the Dogmatic Constitution on Divine Revelation), and *Gaudium et Spes* (the Pastoral Constitution on the Church in the World of Today), as well as the extremely important *Dignitatis Humanae* (the Declaration on Religious Freedom).[27] The entire body of conciliar documents forms the immediate and indispensable context for interpreting *Nostra Aetate*.[28] Among these documents, the four constitutions prove the most central for the Catholic Church's self-understanding. Declarations, such as *Nostra Aetate* and *Dignitatis Humanae*, address particular issues.

## Sacrosanctum Concilium

For most Catholics, the most intimate contact with church life and teaching comes in the liturgy. Prior to the Second Vatican Council, the scripture readings for the Roman Rite of the Mass consisted principally of New Testament readings; there were relatively few selections from the First Testament of the Catholic Bible. *Sacrosanctum Concilium*, the first document issued by Vatican II, instructed that more readings from the Bible be included in the Mass.[29] In accordance with this directive, the revised Roman Rite of the Mass promulgated by Pope Paul VI in 1969 would include a large portion of readings from the First Testament during the liturgical year. For the vast majority of Catholics, this development meant a far greater exposure to the Jewish heritage of Christianity.

## Lumen Gentium

The first conciliar document to express the Catholic Church's view of followers of other religions was *Lumen Gentium* (the Dogmatic Constitution on the Church), issued on November 21, 1964. This constitution strongly affirms the universal salvific will of God operative among all human communities. In sharp contrast to earlier Catholic teaching, *Lumen Gentium* refers positively to the Jewish people as "a people according to their election most dear because of their ancestors: for God never goes back on his gifts and his calling (see Rm 11:28–29)."[30] This affirmation overturns the age-old Catholic belief that God had rejected the Jews because of their rejection of Jesus. Regarding Muslims, *Lumen Gentium* quietly drops the traditional attitude of hostility, stating that "the plan of salvation also embraces those who acknowledge the Creator, and among these the Muslims are first; they profess to hold the faith of Abraham and along with us they worship the one merciful God who will judge humanity on the last day."[31] Instead of linking Muslims to the Antichrist and the Son of Destruction, *Lumen Gentium* includes them in the salvific plan of God, affirming that Muslims worship the one true God in continuity with the faith of Abraham and that they await the final judgment.

## *Dei Verbum*

*Dei Verbum* (the Dogmatic Constitution on Divine Revelation), promulgated on November 18, 1965, reflects on God's revelation of Godself and God's will for the salvation of all humankind.[32] This dogmatic constitution views the Bible both as inspired by God and also as truly written by human authors according to the literary genres of their time. To understand the biblical message willed by God "for the sake of our salvation," *Dei Verbum* urges attention to the literary genres in their historical and cultural context, as well as to the social conventions of the biblical era.[33] The encouragement of literary and historical critical scholarship would have tremendous implications for Catholics interpreting the Bible in relation to the Jewish people both past and present. Today Catholic biblical scholars work in close and frequent collaboration with Jewish scholars in interpreting biblical texts. Increasingly, Catholics read the New Testament texts as Jewish documents that reflect the diversity and conflicts of Judaism in the first century C.E.

## *Gaudium et Spes* and *Dignitatis Humanae*

On December 7, 1965, Pope Paul VI and the Council promulgated *Gaudium et Spes* (the Pastoral Constitution on the Church in the Modern World).[34] Its famous opening words express solidarity with the joys and hopes, the sorrows and anxieties of all people, "especially of those who are poor and afflicted."[35] The constitution forcefully affirms human dignity: "The outstanding feature of human dignity is that human beings have been called to communion with God."[36] In a remarkable admission, the constitution acknowledges that the behavior of some Catholic believers contributed to the rise of modern atheism: "And no small part in the rise of atheism is attributable to believers who may be described more as concealing the true features of God and religion than as revealing them"; *Gaudium et Spes* recognizes that faults in the "religious, moral and social lives" of Catholics have provided some basis for the critique of religion by modern atheists.[37]

*Gaudium et Spes* teaches that through the incarnation, Jesus Christ has united himself to every human being; God's offer of grace is strictly universal in that "the Holy Spirit offers everyone the possibility of sharing in this paschal mystery in a manner known to God."[38] The Second Vatican Council sees the relation of Catholics to followers of other religious paths and to nonbelievers not as the relation of the saved to the unsaved, but rather as the relation between those explicitly acknowledging the grace of God in Jesus Christ and those on other paths who are implicitly touched by the grace of God given in Jesus Christ.

*Dignitatis Humanae* (the Declaration on Religious Freedom), promulgated on the same day as *Gaudium et Spes*, notes the increasing respect for human dignity and the demand that all humans "should enjoy the use of their own responsible judgment and freedom . . . above all with the free and public practice of religion."[39] Recognizing that all humans have an obligation to seek and follow the truth as they understand it, *Dignitatis Humanae* teaches that "truth imposes itself solely by the force of its own truth, as it enters the mind at once gently and with power."[40] The declaration affirms: "This Vatican synod declares that the human person has a right to religious freedom."[41] For the first time in its history, the Catholic Church recognizes the right of all individuals to follow their conscience in freedom in religious matters. The declaration continues: "The practice of religion of its very nature consists principally in internal acts that are voluntary and free, in which one relates oneself to God directly; and these can neither be commanded nor prevented by any merely human power."[42] Though highly controversial at the time, this principle now lies at the center of Catholic teaching and policy in relations with governments and other religious traditions. While remaining deeply rooted in continuity with the Catholic tradition, Vatican II embraced forcefully the principle that the Church can develop and change. Regarding the discussion of religious liberty at Vatican II, Cardinal Bea said, "This is not traditional teaching, but life today is not traditional."[43]

## Nostra Aetate

On October 28, 1965, Pope Paul VI and the Council issued *Nostra Aetate*.[44] The Latin title is *Declaratio de ecclesiae habitudine ad religiones non-christianas* (Declaration on the Church's Relation to Non-Christian

Religions). The topic is the Church's *habitudo*, usually translated as "relation" but which can also mean "attitude." The reference to other religions as "non-christianas" reflects the Vatican usage at the time; the preceding year, in 1964, Pope Paul VI had established the new Secretariat for Non-Christians. This term is problematic in that it refers to other religions by what they are not. This practice would change some years after the Council, in 1988, when the name of the Secretariat for non-Christians (*pro non-christianis*) would become the Pontifical Council for Interreligious Dialogue (PCID).

The opening words *Nostra Aetate*, signal the Council's attention to the signs of the times. As in *Gaudium et Spes* (4), the Council Fathers relate the heritage of the Catholic Church to current developments, especially the more frequent and intense contacts among peoples and nations. "In our age, when the human race is being daily brought closer together and contacts between the various nations are becoming more frequent, the church is giving closer attention to what is its relation to non-christian religions."[45] This implies that our age ("nostra aetas") differs from earlier ages. The "closer attention" will mean a quiet reversal of many earlier attitudes and relations. Usually conciliar documents cite earlier church councils and papal statements, but from nineteen centuries of Catholic history, *Nostra Aetate* will cite only a single papal letter from the eleventh century, and one conciliar document, *Lumen Gentium*.

*Nostra Aetate* primarily focuses on "quae hominibus sunt communia et ad mutuum consortium ducunt" (what things human beings have in common and what things tend to bring them together).[46] It continues the project of Pope John XXIII—aware of the dangers and divisions confronting humans, including the role of religion in fomenting hostility, but seeking grounds for hope and common action. The declaration does not intend to offer a complete statement either on the other religions or on Catholic relations to them.

So what do we have in common? The traditional Catholic teaching that God is the beginning and end of all things provides the Council Fathers a way of naming the broadest context of human life. In a daring statement, the Council Fathers assert: "Una enim communitas sunt omnes gentes" (All nations [or peoples] are one community).[47] To those who believe in inevitable clashes of religions or civilizations, this claim may appear naive, utopian, even counterfactual. The Council Fathers are writing only twenty years after World War II and the Shoah, in the middle of the Cold War, not long after the serious threat of large-scale nuclear war. The world's population is starkly divided into opposing camps, and yet they affirm all peoples as "una communitas." At root, this is a theological assertion. Starting from the traditional Catholic belief that God is the ultimate origin and final end of all creatures, the Council stresses the universal extent of God's providence, goodness, and plan for salvation: all humans are one community because we all share a common origin and also a common vocation to salvation.[48] The assertion of one community among all peoples can also be read as a hopeful proposal of what could become a self-fulfilling prophecy: if all humans believe that we are one community, we will live in accord with this belief and actualize it.

The second section notes a variety of religious answers to the universal question of meaning, commenting that throughout the centuries there has been "a certain perception of that unseen force which is present in the course of things and in events in human life, and sometimes even an acknowledgement of a supreme deity or even of a Father. This perception and acknowledgement permeates their lives with a deep religious sense."[49] Instead of dismissing other religions as superstitious, idolatrous, and pagan, *Nostra Aetate* looks for a point of contact in this "deep religious sense," however variously it may be expressed.

*Nostra Aetate* singles out certain religions "associated with the development of civilization" (religiones vero cum progressu culturae connexae) that seek to respond to human questions "with more refined ideas and more highly developed language."[50] This possibly alludes to Karl Jaspers's famous notion of the Axial Age.[51] The declaration goes on to mention two religions as examples: Hinduism and Buddhism, with very brief descriptions of each: "Thus in Hinduism the divine mystery is explored with an inexhaustible wealth of myths and penetrating philosophical investigations, and liberation is sought from the distresses of our state either through various forms of ascetical life or deep meditation or taking refuge in God with loving confidence."[52] Without making any explicit value judgment, *Nostra Aetate* observes or alludes to various aspects of Hindu life, ranging from the proliferation of mythology to the philosophical tradition, from the practice of yoga to the devotional tradition of bhakti. There is no mention of the Dalit (formerly "untouchable") or the Adivasi (tribal) communities in India.

*Nostra Aetate* then remarks on the variety of forms of Buddhism, alluding to the First Noble Truth of the Buddha and the path to liberation and enlightenment: "In Buddhism, according to its various forms, the radical inadequacy of this changeable world is acknowledged and a way is taught whereby those with a devout and trustful spirit may be able to reach either a state of perfect freedom or, relying on their own efforts or on help from a higher source, the highest illumination."[53] The declaration alludes to the distinction between "self-power" and "Other-power" in some forms of Mahayana Buddhism as paths leading to "summam illuminationem" (the highest illumination). These brief descriptions of the Hindu and Buddhist paths obviously do not intend comprehensiveness but seek only to evoke some significant aspects of these traditions. The document goes on to note that many other religions propose various "ways" (*vias*) to relieve human anxiety, including teachings, rules, and sacred rites.

*Nostra Aetate* does not assess how successful these perspectives and practices are, but it views them with respectful appreciation. What is most distinctive is the benign attitude, the cordial *habitudo* that the Council expresses to these traditions. Instead of earlier Catholic condemnations, the declaration asserts: "The catholic church rejects nothing of those things which are true and holy [vera et sacra] in these religions. It regards with respect those ways of acting and living and those precepts and teachings which, though often at variance with what it holds and expounds, frequently reflect a ray of that truth which enlightens everyone."[54] While the Catholic Church had long acknowledged elements of truth outside the Church based on the natural knowledge of God accessible to all humans, this text goes beyond any previous conciliar statement to acknowledge holiness as well. In Catholic teaching, humans on our own cannot reach a state of holiness because of original sin. Holiness in Catholic theology is a response to divine grace. While the declaration does not take a position on the role of the other religious traditions in the economy of salvation, *Nostra Aetate* does imply that grace reaches humans in and through these other traditions.

This section concludes with a call to all Catholics to participate in dialogue and cooperation with followers of other religions "to recognize, preserve and promote those spiritual and moral good things as well as the socio-cultural values which are to be found among them."[55] It constitutes the charter for Catholic participation in interreligious dialogues and collaborative ventures and has had a tremendous impact in transforming Catholic relations with other traditions.

The next section expresses the respect of the Catholic Church for Muslims. After centuries of Catholic demonizing of Muslims,[56] such words signal a profound shift in attitude. The declaration makes no mention of the Qur'an or Muhammad. *Nostra Aetate* calls attention to the close relation of Muslims to elements of the Catholic faith. In contrast to those who believe Muslims worship a different god, *Nostra Aetate* follows *Lumen Gentium* in teaching that Muslims worship the one true God. It also acknowledges with appreciation Muslims' veneration for Abraham, Jesus, and Mary, and their expectation of a final resurrection and judgment, as well as their practice of prayer, fasting, and almsgiving, three of the Five Pillars of Islam.[57] Passing over most earlier papal statements in silence, the declaration cites a cordial letter from Pope Gregory VII to Al-Nasir, the Muslim ruler of Bijaya, in present-day Algeria, in 1076.[58] This makes for the only reference in *Nostra Aetate* to an earlier papal document; there are no references to earlier ecumenical councils. Regarding the Catholic Church's long history of conflict with Muslims, *Nostra Aetate* proposes that Catholics and Muslims pursue reconciliation through forgetting their past animosity ("praeterita obliviscentes"), so that they can together collaborate in realizing values important to both traditions.

The fourth section is the longest, discussing relations with Jews and Judaism and radically revising centuries of Catholic teaching about the Jewish people.[59] The Council Fathers pass over the long history of negative patristic, papal, and conciliar statements about Jews in silence and instead cite chapters 9 to 11 of Paul's Letter to the Romans as teaching that God's gifts to the Jewish people are irrevocable, *sine paenitentia*, without regret. This means that the covenant God made with ancient Israel has not been broken off, and that Jews should not be viewed as rejected or accursed by God, for they are still God's beloved people. *Nostra Aetate* acknowledges that Catholics receive the Old Testament from the Jewish people and urges Catholics and Jews to cooperate in biblical and theological studies to promote mutual knowledge.[60]

*Nostra Aetate* does not mention the word "deicide," which had been included in an earlier draft and which proved a source of major controversy; but the declaration clearly and forcefully rejects the traditional Catholic practice of collectively blaming Jews of all times and places for the death of Jesus.[61] The declaration notes that while Jewish authorities sought the death of Jesus Christ, "still those things which were perpetrated during his passion cannot be ascribed indiscriminately [indistincte] to all the Jews living at the time nor to the Jews of today."[62] The Council condemns all forms of persecution and deplores anti-Semitism from any source at any time. While the document does not explicitly mention earlier popes and councils, anyone familiar with Catholic Church history knows that this condemnation encompasses a wide array of earlier Catholic teachings and practices.[63]

The fifth section is closely connected to *Dignitatis Humanae* (the Declaration on Religious Freedom), emphasizing the connection between love of God and respect for all humans: "The church therefore condemns as foreign to the mind of Christ any kind of discrimination whatsoever between people, or harassment of them, done by reason of race or colour, class or religion."[64]

Many earlier Catholic Church councils had issued harsh condemnations of those outside the Catholic fold; the Second Vatican Council issued no anathemas, no denunciations, no condemnations, but instead issued an appeal to work together. John O'Malley terms the style of Vatican II "poetic-rhetorical," in contrast to the "legislative-juridical" style that had largely dominated earlier ecumenical councils; he sees Vatican II as deploying a "soft rhetoric" in contrast to the rhetoric of repudiation and condemnation of much earlier Catholic discourse. He describes Vatican II's way of handling the earlier papal condemnations of modernity: "Its strategy was to reject them silently, as if they had never happened."[65] This strategy is at work in *Nostra Aetate*, which, with exception of Gregory VII's letter to Al-Nasir, nowhere mentions any of the many earlier papal and conciliar statements regarding Jews or Muslims. O'Malley's comments about the use of the epideictic genre in the overall rhetorical strategy of the Council apply in particular to *Nostra Aetate*: "The epideictic genre as part of the rhetorical tradition is a form of the art of persuasion, and thus of reconciliation. . . . This genre reminds people of what they have in common rather than of what might divide them, and the reminder motivates them to cooperate on enterprises more important than their divisions. To engage in persuasion is to some extent to put oneself on the same level as those being persuaded."[66]

The rhetoric of *Nostra Aetate* toward other religious traditions seeks reconciliation, cooperation, and collaboration in pursuit of common values in a shared world threatened by numerous dangers. The Second Vatican Council provided a new context for Catholic interreligious relations by expressing an unprecedented degree of respect for other religions, by affirming the right of all people to religious freedom, by recognizing the presence of God's grace in the lives of followers of other religions, by acknowledging the failures and sins of Catholics, and by recognizing the continuing covenantal relationship of God with the Jewish people.

## Effects of the Second Vatican Council on Catholic Interreligious Relations

So where are we today, fifty years after the opening of the Second Vatican Council? As we have seen, *Nostra Aetate* boldly proclaims that all peoples are "one community." One could easily dismiss this statement as naive, impossible, unrealistic, an illusion of the 1960s. As an empirical claim, it can easily be rejected. Pope Benedict XVI, in his Post-Synodal Apostolic Exhortation, *Ecclesia in Medio Oriente* (the Church in the Middle East), which he signed in Lebanon on September 14, 2012, laments the present situation in the Middle East: "How sad it is to see this blessed land suffer in its children who relentlessly tear one another to pieces and die!"[67] Despite the raging conflicts, the Vatican Council's affirmation of one human community remains a Catholic theological belief, grounded not in empirical observation but in the faith that God created all humans and that all humans have a vocation to union with God. The proclamation of this belief by the Council has helped spur interreligious quests for greater understanding and better relations.

## Respect and Reconciliation

Today we face an ambiguous interreligious situation. On the one hand, since October 1962, much has changed for the better. The Second Vatican Council, with its vision of one community, has played a decisive role in transforming Catholic relationships with all other religious traditions. The positive effects are far too numerous to recount here in full. Pope John Paul II demonstrated the implications of the Council for interreligious relations in a number of dramatic actions. On April 13, 1986, he made the first recorded visit of any pope to the Great Synagogue in Rome. John Paul acknowledged and lamented the age-old abuses of Jews by Christians, condemning "acts of discrimination, unjustified limitations of religious freedom, and oppressive restriction of civil freedom as well. . . . Yes, once again, speaking through me the Church deplores, in the words of *Nostra Aetate*, the hatreds, the persecutions, and all the manifestations of anti-Semitism directed against the Jews at any time by whomever."[68] The pope paused, looked directly at the assembly, and stated: "I repeat, by whomever." That obviously included earlier Catholic leaders. In his visit John Paul also stated that Judaism is intrinsic to the Catholic faith.

Later that year, in October, Pope John Paul offered an image of what "una communitas" looks like when he invited leaders of the world's religious traditions to come to Assisi and pray for world peace. As leaders of a wide array of religious traditions gathered, Pope John Paul II made a distinction; he observed that so many diverse traditions could not make a common prayer together, "but we can be present while others pray."[69] He regarded every genuine prayer as inspired by the Holy Spirit. Such an interreligious assembly convoked by a pope would have been unthinkable any time prior to 1960.

As we have seen, *Gaudium et Spes* acknowledged that Catholics had not always acted in ways reflecting the Gospel of Jesus Christ, but had at times concealed the divine message by their improper behavior.[70] In 1994, Pope John Paul II demonstrated the implications of this acknowledgment in his call for a "Purification of Memory" in preparation for the year 2000, asking Catholics to seek God's forgiveness for sins committed against followers of other religious traditions.[71] A few years later, in 1998, the Holy See's Commission for Religious Relations with the Jews issued "We Remember: A Reflection on the Shoah," which observed:

> The history of relations between Jews and Christians is a tormented one. His Holiness Pope John Paul II has recognized this fact in his repeated appeals to Catholics to see where we stand with regard to our relations with the Jewish people. In effect, the balance of these relations over two thousand years has been quite negative. . . . We deeply regret the errors and failures of those sons and daughters of the Church. We make our own what is said in the Second Vatican Council's Declaration *Nostra Aetate*, which unequivocally affirms: "The Church . . . mindful of her common patrimony with the Jews, and motivated by the Gospel's spiritual love and by no political considerations, deplores the hatred, persecutions and displays of anti-Semitism directed against the Jews at any time and from any source."[72]

While many Jewish observers lamented that this statement did not go further in acknowledging failures on the part of the Church itself (not just the "sons and daughters"), it nonetheless constituted a major admission.[73] In the spring of 2000, Pope John Paul journeyed to Jerusalem and prayed at the Western Wall, the most sacred place of prayer for the Jewish people. Following the Jewish custom, he inserted a written prayer into a crack in the wall, asking God's forgiveness for the horrible crimes that Catholics and others have committed against the Jewish people. Aharon Lopez, the ambassador of Israel to the Holy See, commented that the pope deeply moved the Jewish people with this gesture because it entered into the Jewish tradition with respect: "By following the Jewish tradition, he won the hearts of Israelis."[74]

A year later, on May 6, 2001, John Paul II became the first pope ever recorded to visit a mosque—the Umayyad Mosque in Damascus, built on an earlier Byzantine Christian church honoring the grave of St. John the Baptist. John Paul II said: "It is my ardent hope that Muslim and Christian religious leaders and teachers will present our two great religious communities as communities in respectful dialogue, never more as communities in conflict. It is crucial for the young to be taught the ways of respect and understanding, so that they will not be led to misuse religion itself to promote or justify hatred and violence. . . . In Syria, Christians and Muslims have lived side by side for centuries, and a rich dialogue of life has gone on unceasingly. . . . For all the times that Muslims and Christians have offended one another, we need to seek forgiveness from the Almighty and offer each other forgiveness."[75]

Today there exist respectful and friendly relationships between Catholics and followers of other religious paths in many areas on local, national, and international levels; there is now an interreligious community, a network of Catholic interreligious relationships in the United States and around the world on a level that simply did not exist in 1962.[76] Catholic theologians engage in theological discussions with representatives of other religions on an unprecedented level. Catholic colleges and universities sponsor many academic institutes and programs for interreligious study and cooperation. Much more could be said in this regard, and it would indeed prove pleasant to close our narrative here on a positive note. Yet a number of difficulties and obstacles remain as well.

## Challenges

Misunderstandings have challenged Catholic interreligious relationships. In 1994, many Buddhists took offense at Pope John Paul II's comments in "Crossing the Threshold of Hope"; as a result, Theravada Buddhists boycotted his visit to Sri Lanka shortly after the book appeared.[77] A number of Buddhist scholars wrote critical responses, seeking to correct the pontiff's view of Buddhism.[78] The Pontifical Council for Interreligious Dialogue (PCID) proceeded with plans already under way for the first international Colloquium between Buddhists and the Holy See, held at Fo Kuang Shan Monastery in Taiwan in August 1995. This led to the first official joint statement on Buddhist-Catholic relations. The pope's comments in "Crossing the Threshold" expressed his own personal views and were not in any way formal Catholic teaching; the joint statement gives voice to the official Catholic view of Buddhist-Catholic relations. It is to my knowledge the first official Catholic statement in history to be coauthored by Catholic and Buddhist leaders. A later Buddhist-Christian colloquium organized by the PCID in Bangalore, India, in 1998, developed the conversation further in "Word and Silence in Buddhist and Christian Tradition."[79]

Muslims vigorously protested Pope Benedict's remarks regarding Islam in his academic address in Regensburg, Germany, in September 2006.[80] In the wake of widespread furor in the Islamic world, Benedict did not publicly apologize, but he did add explanatory endnotes to the address on the Vatican website, commenting on his quotation from a medieval Christian that had given the greatest offence: "This sentence does not express my personal view of the Qur'an, for which I have the respect due to the holy book of a great religion."[81] Later that fall, a dramatic visual image helped transform the situation. In November 2006, Benedict went to Istanbul, where he stood next to an imam in the Blue Mosque facing toward Mecca, and some Muslims interpreted him as praying in the direction of Mecca.[82]

Perhaps most remarkable was a later development. In October 2007, 138 Muslim leaders from a wide range of Islamic traditions issued an unprecedented address to Pope Benedict and to all Christians, "A Common Word between Us and You."[83] In response, Muslim-Christian dialogues have been held at the Vatican, at Cambridge University, Yale University, and at Georgetown University.[84] These discussions continue. If processed appropriately, misunderstandings can sometimes lead to deeper dialogue and appreciation.

Other challenges arise from the doctrinal claims of the Catholic Church. Popes John Paul II and Benedict XVI have continued Pope Gregory XVI's concern over "indifferentism," now usually termed "relativism."[85] In 2000, the Congregation for the Doctrine of the Faith issued a declaration, "Dominus Iesus: On the Unicity and Salvific Universality of Jesus Christ and the Church," asserting that the Catholic Church alone offers the full mediation of God's gift of salvation through Jesus Christ. The declaration acknowledges that divine grace is offered to followers of other religious paths and that other religions can play a positive role in preparing for salvation. Nonetheless, the statement warns: "If it is true that the followers of other religions can receive divine grace, it is also certain that *objectively speaking* they are in a gravely deficient situation in comparison with those who, in the Church, have the fullness of the means of salvation."[86] Many other Christians and followers of some other religious traditions took offense. The late Jewish theologian Michael Signer exclaimed: "Our whole tedious work of reconstruction after the Council has been shattered with one blow. Jewish-Christian relations are in shambles!"[87] Yet not all dialogue partners reacted in the same way. I was involved in the U.S. Midwest Dialogue of Catholics and Muslims at the time, and my Muslim colleagues in that forum did not object to the declaration, because they held a similar belief from the point of view of Islam. Vatican officials have warned or disciplined Catholic theologians who have not clearly affirmed the unique character of Jesus Christ as savior of all humankind.[88]

Often the most daunting challenges to Catholic interreligious relationships come from religiously motivated violence, persecution, and the violation of religious freedom and human rights. John Allen Jr. wrote in the *National Catholic Reporter*: "According to the International Society for Human Rights, 80 percent of all acts of religious discrimination in the world today are directed at Christians, making Christianity by far the most persecuted religious community on the planet. Reliable estimates say that about 150,000 Christians are killed for the faith every year, which translates into seventeen new martyrs every hour of every day."[89] Numerous areas prove problematic here.

In India today tensions exist between Catholics and some Hindus who have made accusations of forced conversion to Christianity, including the Catholic Church.[90] Most Indian Catholics come from the Dalit or tribal (Adivasi) communities.[91] Some Hindus, especially those involved in the nationalist Hindutva movement, accuse Catholics and other Christians of exploiting the ignorance and poverty of these communities and enticing or even forcing them to convert.[92] In a number of places throughout India, there have been violent attacks by Hindus on Catholics, notably in 2007 and 2008 in the district of Kandhamal in the state of Orissa.[93] In March 2009, an ecumenical assembly of virtually all the Christian communities in India issued a dramatic appeal for the world's attention and support for the Indian Christians suffering violence.[94] Indian Catholic leaders insist that conversions to the Catholic Church are a free choice and are not coerced.

An atmosphere of distrust still hovers today in some areas of India. A recent article in the *Union of Catholic Asian News* (UCAN) proclaims: "Four Years Later, Fear Still Stalks Orissa: Kandhamal Christians Still Live in Fear."[95] Reports of attacks by Hindus on Christians continue.[96] The Message of the Holy See to Hindus for the Feast of Deepavali in October 2011 expresses concern for religious freedom: "Maintaining our tradition of sharing a reflection on this occasion, we propose this year the theme of Religious Freedom. This subject is currently taking center stage in many places, calling our attention to those members of our human family exposed to bias, prejudice, hate propaganda, discrimination and persecution on the basis of religious affiliation. Religious freedom is the answer to religiously motivated conflicts in many parts of the world. Amid the violence triggered by these conflicts, many desperately yearn for peaceful coexistence and integral human development. . . . Moreover, it [religious freedom] includes the freedom to change one's own religion. "[97]

In Sri Lanka, some Buddhists have attacked Christians and Christian churches. In 2012, there were reports of about fifty attacks by Buddhists against various Christian denominations; Rayyappu Joseph, the Catholic bishop of Mannar, was injured in one of the assaults. A group called Bodu Bala Sena (Buddhist Power Force) has called on Buddhists to defend Sri Lanka from Christians and Muslims.[98] In these contexts, the affirmation of universal religious freedom, which popes prior to Vatican II had firmly rejected, has paradoxically become the cornerstone of Catholic interreligious relations today.

Religious freedom is also a major concern in Muslim-Catholic relations. In a number of Muslim-majority nations, conflicts arise between Muslims and Christians. There have been repeated violent attacks against Catholics and other Christians, as well as difficulties regarding laws concerning blasphemy and apostasy. Pope Benedict and other Catholic leaders have shown acute awareness of the fact that Catholics and other Christian communities in the Middle East have suffered much in the past seventy years; many have left their homelands, which threatens the very existence of Christian populations in some regions.[99] Pope Benedict and other Catholic leaders repeatedly condemned religiously motivated violence and discrimination from whatever source, and they have insisted on respect for religious freedom for all. For the feast of Eid al-Fitr at the end of Ramadan in 2012, Louis Cardinal Tauran, the president of PCID, sent Muslims a message of cordial greetings, which concluded: "Christians and Muslims are too often witnesses to the violation of the sacred, of the mistrust of which those who call themselves believers are the target. We cannot but denounce all forms of fanaticism and intimidation, the prejudices and the polemics, as well as the discrimination of which, at times, believers are the object both in the social and political life as well as in the mass media. We are spiritually very close to you, dear Friends, asking God to give you renewed spiritual energy and we send you our very best wishes for peace and happiness."[100]

In October 2010, Pope Benedict convened a Special Assembly of the Synod of Bishops to discuss "The Catholic Church in the Middle East: Communion and Witness." In his Post-Synodal Apostolic Exhortation, *Ecclesia in Medio Oriente*, Benedict proclaimed: "Religious freedom is the pinnacle of all other freedoms. It is a sacred and inalienable right. It includes on the individual and collective levels the freedom to follow one's conscience in religious matters and, at the same time, freedom of worship."[101] Benedict called on Jews and Muslims to join with Christians in rejecting what he calls "a violent fundamentalism claiming to be based on religion."[102] The threatened, precarious position of Catholics and other

Christians in many Muslim-majority states makes for a serious challenge in Catholic-Muslim relations today.

From before the time of the Second Vatican Council to the present, the unresolved Israeli-Palestinian conflict has constituted an enormous challenge to Jewish-Catholic relations on multiple levels. Even though the Second Vatican Council did not directly address the question of relations between the State of Israel and the Holy See, it nonetheless prepared the way for diplomatic relations.[103] On December 30, 1993, Vatican and Israeli representatives signed the Fundamental Agreement between the Holy See and the State of Israel. This led to the establishment of full diplomatic relations in 1994. Through this agreement the Holy See recognizes the government of Israel, but the Israeli Knesset has never approved the legislation to implement the Fundamental Agreement. There remain many issues unresolved between the Catholic Church and the State of Israel, including disputes over ownership of land and the status of the Catholic Church in Israel.[104]

In 2009, Palestinian Catholic leaders together with other Christian leaders in the Holy Land issued a forceful statement called *Kairos Palestine*, which presents itself as "a cry of hope."[105] "Kairos" is the Greek word used in the New Testament to designate a special time of opportunity; in 1985 a group of black South African theologians issued the *Kairos Document* in protest against the system of apartheid. The former Latin Patriarch of Jerusalem, Archbishop Michel Sabbah, served as one of the drafters and signers. The Latin Patriarch of Jerusalem and bishops from the Armenian Catholic, Syrian Catholic, and Greek Catholic Churches signed a separate statement, publicly disseminated both in hard copy and online as the "Preamble" of the declaration. This suggests an informal endorsement of the concerns of the statement. Like the Melkite Synod in August 1962, the *Kairos Palestine* statement rejects any interpretation of the Bible that would justify the conquest and confiscation of land: "We also declare that the Israeli occupation of Palestinian land is a sin against God and humanity because it deprives the Palestinians of their basic human rights, bestowed by God. It distorts the image of God in the Israeli who has become an occupier just as it distorts this image in the Palestinian living under occupation."[106] The document gives expression to the anguish that arises from extreme frustration: "Why now? Because today we have reached a dead end in the tragedy of the Palestinian people."[107] The document further asserts: "Palestinians within the State of Israel, who have suffered a historical injustice, although they are citizens and have the rights and obligations of citizenship, still suffer from discriminatory policies. They too are waiting to enjoy full rights and equality like all other citizens in the state."[108] The situation of Catholics and other Christians in Israel and Palestine remains an extremely difficult, unresolved tension in Catholic-Jewish relations.[109]

## Pope Francis

On March 13, 2013, the Conclave of Cardinals of the Catholic Church elected Jorge Mario Cardinal Bergoglio as the 266th Pope. As the archbishop of Buenos Aires, he had long been involved in discussions with his friend Rabbi Abraham Skorka, and they had published a book presenting their conversations, *On Heaven and Earth*.[110] Introducing the dialogue, Bergoglio refers to an image on the façade of the cathedral in Buenos Aires of the biblical Joseph embracing his brothers in Egypt after many years of separation and estrangement; Bergoglio finds in this image of Joseph and his brothers an invitation to establish a "culture of encounter." As we have seen, *Dominus Iesus* ominously warns that all followers of other religions are "in a gravely deficient situation" regarding their salvation; Cardinal Bergoglio set a rather different tone in offering a beautiful description of the attitude required for genuine dialogue: "Dialogue is born from a respectful attitude toward the other person, from a conviction that the other person has something good to say. It supposes that we can make room in our heart for their point of view, their opinion and their proposals. Dialogue entails a warm reception and not a preemptive condemnation. To dialogue, one must know how to lower the defenses, to open the doors of one's home and to offer warmth" (xiv).

We have seen that *Nostra Aetate* affirms a universal religious quest for God, which contains elements of truth and holiness; Bergoglio develops this theme as he affirms: "God makes Himself felt in the heart of each person. He also respects the culture of all people. Each nation picks up that vision of God and translates it in accordance with the culture, and elaborates, purifies and gives it a system. Some cultures are primitive in their explanations, but God is open to all people. He calls everyone. He moves everyone to seek Him and to discover Him through creation" (19).

After Pope Benedict XVI's comments regarding Islam in the speech in Regensburg, Cardinal Bergoglio's spokesman commented on his behalf: "Pope Benedict's statements don't reflect my own opinions." He added: "These statements will serve to destroy in twenty seconds the careful construction of a relationship with Islam that Pope John Paul II built over the last twenty years."[111] In an effort to mend relations, for the celebration of Ramadan in 2013, Pope Francis decided to send the annual message from the Catholic Church to the worldwide Islamic community as his personal greeting, as a sign of the importance that he places on Muslim-Catholic relations.[112]

On November 24, 2013, Pope Francis issued an Apostolic Exhortation, the first of his pontificate, and the first major statement of his program.[113] The great theme of Pope Francis's exhortation found expression in the title: *Evangelii Gaudium*, the Joy of the Gospel, which closely resembles the title of Pope John's opening speech in October 1962 to the first session of the Second Vatican Council: *Gaudet Mater Ecclesia*. Francis directly quotes the words of Pope John's speech, rejecting the "prophets of doom" and looking beyond the predictions of gloom to hope: "In our times, divine Providence is leading us to a new order of human relations" (84).

In the exhortation, Pope Francis affirms the special relationship of the Catholic Church to the Jewish people (247), and he reaches out to the Muslim community (252–53). Francis continues the initiative of Vatican II in strongly supporting interreligious initiatives in the context of seeking peace and the flourishing of life for all: "An attitude of openness in truth and in love must characterize the dialogue with the followers of non-Christian religions. . . . Interreligious dialogue is a necessary condition for peace in the world, and so it is a duty for Christians as well as other religious communities" (250). Francis endorses the interreligious attitude commended by the Catholic bishops of India of "being open to them, sharing their joys and sorrows" (250). He also provides the hoped-for result of such an attitude of openness: "In this way we learn to accept others and their different ways of living, thinking and speaking. We can then join one another in taking up the duty of serving justice and peace, which should become a basic principle of all our exchanges. A dialogue which seeks social peace and justice is in itself, beyond all merely practical considerations, an ethical commitment which brings about a new social situation." (250)

Pope Francis acknowledges the important differences among various religious traditions and does not wish to ignore or minimize them: "A facile syncretism would ultimately be a totalitarian gesture on the part of those who would ignore greater values of which they are not the masters. True openness involves remaining steadfast in one's deepest convictions, clear and joyful in one's own identity, while at the same time being 'open to understanding those of the other party' and 'knowing that dialogue can enrich each side'" (250; quoting Pope John Paul II).

## Conclusion

That we live in a time of serious threats and seemingly insurmountable problems would not have surprised the Fathers of the Second Vatican Council. They remembered vividly the devastation of the Second World War, and the Council opened at a time of severe international crisis, when the world was probably the closest in all of history to a large-scale nuclear exchange. The question posed by Jules Isaac to Pope John XXIII in 1960 has echoed through the decades: "Is there reason for hope?" One could easily respond in the negative. There is little prospect that the many interreligious conflicts raging today will be resolved any time in the near future. Obviously, the Catholic Church cannot control the attitudes or behavior of other religious communities, and it would be naive to expect that any one religious body's transformation could resolve the multiple problems of interreligious conflicts.

What the Second Vatican Council did accomplish was dramatically and effectively to change the long-term stance of the Catholic Church in relation to other religions and to religious freedom. Instead of being a prominent and powerful opponent of religious freedom, the Catholic Church today has established itself as one of its most eloquent and insistent defenders. The most significant legacy of the Council for interreligious interactions is the international network of respectful relationships that Catholics now enjoy with followers of other religious traditions. These relationships provide a forum for addressing and responding to the multiple difficulties Catholics face alongside representatives of other traditions.

In Catholic theology, hope is not to be confused with worldly optimism, the expectation or prediction of desired outcomes in this world; instead, hope constitutes a theological virtue that comes as a gift from God. In the Catholic tradition, the virtue of hope seeks a future good, which is arduous but possible to obtain through the grace of God. It is most important precisely when conflicts are most possible. In this sense, the response to Isaac from a hopeful, holy man, Pope John, echoes as well: "You have reason for more than hope."

Continuing the hopeful tone of Pope John amid all the difficulties and challenges facing the global community, Francis encourages us: "Challenges exist to be overcome! Let us be realists, but without losing our joy, our boldness and our hope-filled commitment" (*Evangelii Gaudium*, 109).

NOTES

1. Morselli, "Jules Isaac and the Origins of *Nostra Aetate*," 21–28; Hebblethwaite, *John XXIII: Pope of the Century*, 92.

2. Oesterreicher, "Declaration on the Relationship of the Church to Non-Christian Religions," 2.

3. Ibid., 3.

4. Fisher, "Catholics and Jews: Twenty Centuries and Counting," 106–42.

5. Isaac, *The Teaching of Contempt*; Isaac, *Jesus and Israel*.

6. Connelly, *From Enemy to Brother, 1933–1965*.

7. Oesterreicher, "Declaration on the Relationship of the Church to Non-Christian Religions," 8–17.

8. Connelly, *From Enemy to Brother, 1933–1965*, 5; emphasis in original.

9. Pope Gregory XVI, "Mirari Vos." See also Chadwick, *A History of the Popes 1830–1914*, 23–25.

10. Pope Gregory XVI, "Mirari Vos."

11. Murray, *We Hold These Truths*; Murray, *Religious Liberty*; Nugent, *Silence Speaks*.

12. That is, the Third Lateran Council ordered: "Jews and Saracens are not to be allowed to have Christian servants in their houses." *Canon*, 26, in Tanner, *Decrees of the Ecumenical Councils*, 1:223. See also Second Council of Lyons regarding "the blasphemous and faithless Saracens," in *Constitution*, 1, in Tanner, *Decrees of the Ecumenical Councils*, 1:309.

13. Daniel, *Islam and the West*, 210–12; Palmer and Brock, "The Apocalypse of Pseudo-Methodius," 222–42; Alexander, *The Byzantine Apocalyptic Tradition*; Martinez, "Eastern Christian Apocalyptic in the Early Muslim Period," 58–246; McGinn, *Antichrist*, 150.

14. Reinders, *Borrowed Gods and Foreign Bodies*; Fernando and Gispert-Sauch, *Christianity in India*, 116–20.

15. That is, Jesuits including Matteo Ricci, Roberto de Nobili, Ippolito Desideri, and Alexandre de Rhodes explored other religious traditions with respect.

16. Fries, *Fundamental Theology*, 277–81; Hötzel, *Die Uroffenbarung im französischen Traditionalismus*; Pieper, *Tradition als Herausforderung*.

17. Gibbons, "The Needs of Humanity Supplied by the Catholic Religion," 164.

18. The Apostolic Legate, Archbishop Francesco Satolli, was concerned that Catholic participation meant that the one true Church was simply one among many religions. After receiving his negative report, Pope Leo XIII ordered that if another such event not organized by the Catholic Church was held, Catholics were not to participate. Pope Leo did allow that Catholics could hold their own assemblies and invite "dissenters" to attend. Cleary, "Catholic Participation in the World's Parliament of Religions, Chicago, 1893," 605.

19. The Jesuit Scripture scholar Augustin Bea called for a revised Catholic view of Jews. Louis Massignon wrote major studies of Sufi Islam and pioneered friendly relations with Muslims, even to the point that Pope Pius XI called him "a Catholic Muslim." In India, the Benedictine monks Henri LeSaux (Abhishiktananda) and Bede Griffiths explored the Advaitic and Sannyasi tradition of Hinduism, while in Japan the Jesuit Hugo Enomiya Lassalle was practicing Zen Buddhism and his fellow Jesuit Heinrich Dumoulin was writing a history of Zen Buddhism.

20. Stransky, "The Genesis of *Nostra Aetate*: Surprises, Setbacks, and Blessings"; See also Stransky, "The Genesis of *Nostra Aetate*: An Insider's Story."

21. See Oesterreicher, "Declaration on the Relationship of the Church to Non-Christian Religions," 17–136.

22. Bea insisted on the purely religious, nonpolitical character of the text in addresses to the Council in November 1963, October and November 1964, and November 1965. Bea, *The Church and the Jewish People*, 10, 154, 164, 167, 170.

23. By one count, people used seven different Latin titles before finally arriving at *Declaratio de ecclesiae habitudine ad religiones non-christianas* (Declaration on the Church's Relation to non-Christian Religions) and the famous opening words, *Nostra Aetate*. See Congar, *My Journal of the Council*, 937.

24. Within the Council, Archbishop Marcel Lefebvre was one of the conservative minority who vehemently opposed any change in Catholic teaching concerning the Jewish people, the possibility of Jews being saved without conversion to Catholicism, religious freedom, or the relationship between the Catholic Church and the state. Lefebvre, who was superior general of the Holy Ghost Fathers during Vatican II, represented the monarchist wing of French Catholicism that went back to the French Revolution. This strand of French Catholicism had long opposed the separation of church and state, religious liberty, and modern democracy; instead it called for an absolutist monarchy with union of throne and altar, the Catholic Church resuming its for them rightful place as the established church of France. Lefebvre supported the "Catholic order" of the authoritarian French Vichy regime, which collaborated with the Nazis from 1940 to1944.

25. Shofany, *The Melkites at the Vatican Council II*, 106–7.

26. Abbott, *The Documents of Vatican II*, 712; cited in Kobler, *Vatican II and Phenomenology*, 25; see also Pope John XXIII, "Opening Speech to the Vatican II Council.".

27. O'Collins, *The Second Vatican Council on Other Religions*.

28. Faggioli, *Vatican II*, 125–33; Rush, *Still Interpreting Vatican II*; Gaillardetz and Clifford, *Keys to the Council*.

29. "In order that believers can be provided with a richer diet of God's word, the rich heritage of the Bible is to be opened more widely, in such a way that a fuller and more nourishing selection of the scriptures gets read to the people within a fixed period of years." *Sacrosanctum Concilium*, 51, in Tanner, *Decrees of the Ecumenical Councils*, 2:831.

30. *Lumen Gentium*, 16, in Tanner, *Decrees of the Ecumenical Councils*, 2:861.

31. Ibid.

32. *Dei Verbum*, 6, in Tanner, *Decrees of the Ecumenical Councils*, 2:973. See also Witherup, *Scripture*.

33. *Dei Verbum*, 11–12, in Tanner *Decrees of the Ecumenical Councils*, 2:976. *Dei Verbum* distinguishes among the teaching of Jesus Christ the oral tradition passed on by the apostles and other disciples and the final stage of composition of the canonical gospels, which was done "with a view to the needs of the churches." *Dei Verbum*, 19, in Tanner, *Decrees of the Ecumenical Councils*, 2:978.

34. Tanner, *The Church and the World*.

35. "The joys and hopes and the sorrows and anxieties of people today, especially of those who are poor and afflicted, are also the joys and hopes, sorrows and anxieties of the disciples of Christ, and there is nothing truly human which does not also affect them." *Gaudium et Spes*, 1, in Tanner, *Decrees of the Ecumenical Councils*, 2:1069.

36. *Gaudium et Spes*, 19, in Tanner, *Decrees of the Ecumenical Councils*, 2:1079.

37. Ibid. See also *Gaudium et Spes*, 43, in Tanner, *Decrees of the Ecumenical Councils*, 2:1098.

38. *Gaudium et Spes*, 22, in Tanner, *Decrees of the Ecumenical Councils*, 2:1082.

39. *Dignitatis Humanae*, 1, in Tanner, *Decrees of the Ecumenical Councils*, 2:1002.

40. Ibid.

41. *Dignitatis Humanae*, 2, in Tanner, *Decrees of the Ecumenical Councils*, 2:1002.

42. *Dignitatis Humanae*, 3, in Tanner, *Decrees of the Ecumenical Councils*, 2:1003.

43. O'Malley, *What Happened at Vatican II*, 214.

44. Cassidy, *Ecumenism and Interreligious Dialogue*.

45. *Nostra Aetate*, 1, in Tanner, *Decrees of the Ecumenical Councils*, 2:968.

46. Ibid.

47. Ibid.

48. In the following month, *Gaudium et Spes* would teach that in a way known to God, the Holy Spirit actively offers salvation to all people. See *Gaudium et Spes*, 22, in Tanner, *Decrees of the Ecumenical Councils*, 2:1082.

49. *Nostra Aetate*, 2, in Tanner, *Decrees of the Ecumenical Councils*, 2:969.

50. Ibid.

51. Jaspers, *The Origin and Goal of History*, 1–21.

52. *Nostra Aetate*, 2, in Tanner, *Decrees of the Ecumenical Councils*, 2:969.

53. Ibid.

54. Ibid.

55. Ibid.

56. Daniel, *Islam and the West*.

57. *Nostra Aetate*, 3, in Tanner, *Decrees of the Ecumenical Councils*, 2:969

58. Gregory VII wrote: "Almighty God, who wishes that all should be saved and none lost, approves nothing in us so much as that after loving him one should love his fellow man, and that one should not do to others, what one does not want done to oneself. You and we owe this charity to ourselves especially because we believe in and confess one God, admittedly in a different way, and daily praise and venerate him, the Creator of the world and ruler of this world." Quoted by Pope John Paul II, "Message to the Faithful of Islam at the End of the Month of Ramadan," 66.

59. Bea, *The Church and the Jewish People*, 13–15.

60. *Nostra Aetate*, 4, in Tanner, *Decrees of the Ecumenical Councils*, 2:970.

61. Bea, *The Church and the Jewish People*, 160–62.

62. *Nostra Aetate*, 4, in Tanner, *Decrees of the Ecumenical Councils*, 2:970; Nirenberg, *Anti-Judaism: The Western Tradition*.

63. Flannery, *The Anguish of the Jews*; Nicholls, *Christian Antisemitism*.

64. *Nostra Aetate*, 5; in Tanner, *Decrees of the Ecumenical Councils*, 2:971.

65. O'Malley, "Trent and Vatican II," 312.

66. Ibid., 313.

67. Pope Benedict XVI, "Post-Synodal Apostolic Exhortation *Ecclesia in Medio Oriente*," 31.

68. Bernstein and Politi, *His Holiness*, 443–44.

69. Pope John Paul II, "The Challenge and the Possibility of Peace," 370.

70. *Gaudium et Spes*, 19, in Tanner, *Decrees of the Ecumenical Councils*, 2:1079. See also *Gaudium et Spes*, 43, in Tanner, *Decrees of the Ecumenical Councils*, 2:1098.

71. Pope John Paul II, "Tertio Millennio Adveniente."

72. Cassidy, "We Remember."

73. A conference of Jewish and Catholic leaders at the Catholic Theological Union in Chicago in 1999 reflected on and critiqued the document. See Banki and Pawlikowski, *Ethics in the Shadow of the Holocaust*.

74. Aharon Lopez quoted in Cernera, "The Center for Christian-Jewish Understanding of Sacred Heart University," 154.

75. John Paul II, "Address of the Holy Father."

76. There are distinct units in the Holy See that handle interreligious relations. The Pontifical Council for Interreligious Dialogue (PCID) represents the Holy See in interreligious relations with other religious communities except Jews. There is a separate Pontifical Commission for Religious Relations with Jews, whose President is also the Prefect of the Pontifical Council for Promoting Christian Unity (PCPCU). This framework has its roots in the original request of Pope John XXIII in 1960 that the newly established Secretariat for Christian Unity prepare a statement on Catholic relations with Jews. The Vatican secretary of state handles political and diplomatic relations between the Holy See and the government of Israel.

77. John Paul II, *Crossing the Threshold of Hope*, 84–90.

78. Aitken, "The Intrareligious Realization"; Abe, "On John Paul II's View of Buddhism"; Cabezón, "A Buddhist Response to John Paul II."

79. *Pro Dialogo* 100 (1999.1), 1–185.

80. Pope Benedict cited a medieval conversation reportedly held between the Byzantine Emperor Manuel II Paleologus and an unnamed educated Persian in which Manuel II reportedly charged: "Show me just what Mohammed brought that was new, and there you will find things only evil and inhuman, such as his command to spread by the sword the faith he preached." See Pope Benedict XVI, "Faith, Reason and the University: Memories and Reflections."

81. "In the Muslim world, this quotation has unfortunately been taken as an expression of my personal position, thus arousing understandable indignation. I hope that the reader of my text can see immediately that this sentence does not express my personal view of the Qur'an, for which I have the respect due to the holy book of a great religion. In quoting the text of the Emperor Manuel II, I intended solely to draw out the essential relationship between faith and reason. On this point I am in agreement with Manuel II, but without endorsing his polemic." See Pope Benedict XVI, "Faith, Reason and the University."

82. "Pontiff in Blue Mosque"; "Pope Makes Turkish Mosque Visit."

83. "A Common Word."

84. Borelli, *A Common Word and the Future of Christian-Muslim Relations*.

85. John Paul II, *Redemptoris Missio*, 36; Pope and Hefling, *Dominus Iesus*, 22, in *Sic et Non: Encountering Dominus Iesus*, 21.

86. Pope and Hefling, *Dominus Iesus*, 22, in *Sic et Non: Encountering Dominus Iesus*, 21–22; emphasis in the original.

87. Heinz, "'Your Privilege,'" 11.

88. Regarding Roger Haight, see Haight, "Notification on the Book *Jesus Symbol of God*." Regarding Jacques Dupuis, see Dupuis, "Notification on the Book *Toward a Christian Theology of Religious Pluralism*."

89. Allen, "Real War on Religion and a Ticking Vatican PR bomb."

90. Karlsson, "Entering into the Christian Dharma."

91. According to some estimates, about 65–70 percent of Indian Christians come from a Dalit background, and another 15–20 percent from tribal communities. Robinson and Kujur, *Margins of Faith*, 5.

92. Fernando and Gispert-Sauch, *Christianity in India*, 192; Teltumbde, *Hindutva and Dalits*.

93. Bauman, "Identity, Conversion, and Violence"; Chatterji, *Violent Gods*, 279–363.

94. "Elections 2009."

95. "Four Years Later, Fear Still Stalks Orissa." The Indian Jesuit theologian Vincent Sekhar stresses the vital importance of the secular constitution of the state of India and the separation of religion and government to protect the minority religious communities. Sekhar, *Building Strong Neighbourhood*.

96. Sharma, "Mob Attacks Christians for Playing Hymns."

97. Pontifical Council for Interreligious Dialogue, "Christians and Hindus."

98. "Christian-Buddhist Tensions Turn Violent in Sri Lanka."

99. Pope Benedict XVI, "Post-Synodal Apostolic Exhortation *Ecclesia in Medio Oriente*," 31.

100. "Christians and Muslims."

101. Benedict XVI, "Post-Synodal Apostolic Exhortation *Ecclesia in Medio Oriente*," 26.

102. Ibid.

103. Kenny, *Catholics, Jews, and the State of Israel*.

104. Chacour and Michel, *Faith Beyond Despair*; Chacour and Jensen, *We Belong to the Land*.

105. Kairos Palestine, *Kairos Palestine*, 2; see also www.kairospalestine.ps. Between 1988 and 2008 the Jerusalem Heads of Churches issued sixty-eight joint public statements on the situation of Palestinian Christians in the Holy Land. See May, *Jerusalem Testament*.

106. Kairos Palestine, *Kairos Palestine*, 9.

107. Ibid., 4.

108. Ibid., 5.

109. While some Jews have tended to equate criticism of the State of Israel with anti-Semitism, the declaration of the International Council of Christians and Jews issued in 2009, *A Time for Recommitment: Jewish Christian Dialogue Seventy Years after War and Shoah*, called on Jews: "To differentiate between fair-minded criticism of Israel and anti-Semitism" (18).

110. Bergoglio and Skorka, *On Heaven and Earth*. All further references to this text will appear parenthetically in the running text.

111. Baverstock, "Pope Francis' Run-In with Benedict XVI over the Prophet Mohammed."

112. Pope Francis, "The Message of Pope Francis to Muslims throughout the World for the End of Ramadan ('Id al-Fitr). 10 July 2013."

113. Pope Francis, "Apostolic Exhortation on the Joy of the Gospel (*Evangelii Gaudium*)."

2

# THE AMERICAN RECEPTION AND LEGACY
# OF THE SECOND VATICAN COUNCIL

*Leslie Woodcock Tentler*

Let me begin with a bit of background. The Second Vatican Council met in four sessions in Rome from October 1962 to December 1965. It issued sixteen documents, which taken together represent a judiciously worded repudiation of the militant opposition to modernity that had characterized the papacy since the time of the French Revolution. The Council Fathers endorsed religious liberty and ecumenism, authorized a gradual reform of the Tridentine liturgy, including the use of the vernacular, and embraced a new posture of openness to both the contemporary world and historical-mindedness. In the felicitous words of Father John O'Malley, "liberty, equality and fraternity . . . knocked at the door and gained entrance to the feast."[1] Not many Catholics, then or now, have actually read these documents. Most of what Catholics knew at the time about the Council probably came from the secular media. But thanks to the extent and tenor of that media coverage, most Catholics became aware that this Council represented something new, both in mood and—to invoke O'Malley again—in terms of language. This was a Council without anathemas. Whatever struggles took place behind the scenes, the public face of the Council was winsomely irenic.

The meaning of Vatican II makes for a contentious topic among Catholics today, less because of the Council itself than because of what came after. The Council was called in part to address the declining fortunes of Catholicism in much of continental Europe. But though many Europeans greeted its reforms with enthusiasm, the Council did not succeed in reviving Catholic practice there. Quite to the contrary. Shortly after the Council closed in 1965, Catholic practice began to decline even in those parts of Europe and North America where it had hitherto been robust— in the Netherlands, Spain, Bavaria, and Ireland. The same was precipitously true in Quebec and, more slowly, in the United States. Vocations to the priesthood and religious life in these locales declined even more sharply than attendance at Mass. Catholics in droves abandoned the sacrament of penance—or confession, as it was popularly known—which was the most visible indication of their having rejected not just the legalism of the preconciliar church but its preoccupation with what we used to call the "four last things" (death, judgment, heaven, and hell.) Hell disappeared, to put it succinctly, largely because Catholics, including the clergy, ceased to talk about and seemingly to fear it. In these liberating circumstances, growing numbers of Catholics claimed the right to "decide for themselves" with regard to such matters as birth control, premarital sex, divorce and remarriage, even homosexuality and abortion.

Thus, shortly after the conclusion of the Council, the Catholic Church in the developed world seemed suddenly in disarray. Was the Council itself responsible? Hardly any historians today would answer yes to that question; they generally regard the Council as an accelerant of social processes already well under way at the time the Council began. Indeed, the chief mystery with regard to what followed the Council is not the *direction* of the change that occurred. Catholics in Europe and North America became more like their non-Catholic neighbors, which seems hardly surprising. In places like the Netherlands, Quebec, and the United States plentiful signs before the Council indicated that Catholics were growing impatient with the boundaries—psychological and otherwise—enforced by the subcultures they inhabited. The chief mystery is rather the *speed* with which that change occurred. By 1966, with liturgical reform still in its opening stages, talk was rampant among priests—especially younger priests—about a crisis of identity. Seminary enrollments in that same year began what would soon prove a precipitous decline. (In American seminaries, there had actually been an uptick in enrollment during the Council years.) By 1967, priests had begun to leave the priesthood in significant numbers—not surreptitiously, as had been the norm for the rare priest who left before the Council, but with noisy self-justification. Sisters were leaving the convent in even greater numbers, though usually in quieter fashion, which had swift and devastating impact on Catholic schools, which were closing in large numbers by the early 1970s. Priests documented a decline in confession as early as 1966, by which time Mass attendance had also begun its downward trend. The intra-Catholic debate over birth control went public in 1964, even before the Council had ended. In terms of mood and behavior, the Church by 1968—whether in the United States, Holland, or Quebec—was light years away from its hierarchical and supremely ordered preconciliar self: contentious, deeply polarized, and riddled with uncertainty. Again, this seems hardly surprising.

No institution could endure such rapid change without far-reaching and probably deleterious consequences.

*Why* did the process of postconciliar change prove so rapid? This essay offers some answers to that question, though its conclusions remain inevitably tentative. The reception of the Council, after all, was a complicated business. Catholics in my hometown of Detroit were told to pray that "the decisions of the Council may find in us generous acceptance and prompt fulfillment." We should not pay attention to secular news stories about the Council, we were cautioned in a sermon preached from all local pulpits in 1963; these were invariably incomplete or inaccurate. Instead, "we must wait patiently until we eventually learn, through the voice of our Archbishop, what the Church, our Mother and Teacher, would have us do."[2] Some of our non-Catholic neighbors doubtless imagined that this is indeed how local Catholics would behave, since they knew for a fact that we could not think for ourselves—a sentiment heard frequently in the course of the interconfessional children's squabbles that were so ubiquitous a feature of my religiously mixed neighborhood.

Any bishop, however, could have told you that the prospects were far murkier. A bishop could reasonably expect that his priests would implement the various liturgical reforms on the schedule determined by the U.S. Conference of Catholic Bishops. In this sense, at least, he had an advantage over his sixteenth-century counterpart in the wake of the Council of Trent. But he could not guarantee that all his priests would explain the theology behind the reforms or encourage their congregations to participate in the ritual to the degree that the Council Fathers had envisioned. Every diocese had its liturgical laggards—priests, often older men, who were hostile to the new liturgy and made no effort to hide this from their people. And every diocese had its liturgical radicals. Thus the experience of the new liturgy—the principal means by which Catholics encountered the reforming logic of Vatican II—could and often did vary from one parish to the next. Growing numbers of Catholics responded by shopping around for parishes where they found the liturgy to their liking—a sharp departure from preconciliar practice, when Catholics were strictly forbidden to attach themselves to any but the neighborhood church or a parish intended for members of a particular ethnic group.

The heterogeneity of the American Catholic population also complicated the business of receiving the Council's reforms. Divisions among Catholics by the early 1960s were based less on ethnicity, once the principal source of intra-Catholic tensions, than class. Catholic upward mobility soared after 1945, with the rising generation benefitting enormously from the G.I. Bill and an expanding economy. American Catholics were still a disproportionately working-class group as late as 1945; by the early 1970s, they rivaled mainline Protestants in terms of education and income.[3] What had been a predominantly urban population in 1945 was by the early 1970s a heavily suburban one. Working-class Catholics were suddenly an aging minority in a church whose culture had historically reflected their values and experience.

Class standing did not determine an individual's response to the Council. But it is worth noting that the most zealous lay proponents of the Council's reforms tended overwhelmingly to be young and highly educated. Indeed, the means by which the reforms were instituted in many dioceses—the study clubs and discussion groups, the adult education courses in the new theology—put a premium on participants being articulate, at home with abstractions, and confident with regard to self-presentation. Less-educated Catholics might easily come to feel that the postconciliar church privileged qualities they themselves lacked. This does not mean that large numbers of American Catholics opposed the Council's principal reforms. The vernacular liturgy was broadly popular in this country, where Catholic traditionalism has always been a small fringe movement. The move away from Catholic legalism and its attendant culture of fear proved broadly popular too. I do think, however, that many American Catholics received the Council's reforms in a relatively passive way. If the laity now belonged to the people of God rather than the Church militant, they were willing to accept it on authority.

So the Council impacted American Catholics at different rates and in different ways. And this meant tension, even polarization, as some moved faster than others and sometimes in directions that could hardly have been anticipated by the Council Fathers. Forces and circumstances that had little to do with the Council itself also mediated its impact. Only limited segments of the American Catholic population responded to the Council with an immediate alteration in discourse and practice. But because these early changers were highly visible—their numbers came mainly from the younger clergy and lay veterans of the various Catholic Action movements—they often precipitated change, or at least reaction, among Catholics more generally. It was not easy to ignore a Young Turk priest in one's parish, especially if he favored liturgical experimentation, while many Catholic publications were increasingly oriented to the altered consciousness of the activist laity. Change fed on itself, in other words, and in ways not immediately predictable. Beyond this dynamic, and even more important, were the particular historical circumstances in which American Catholics received the Council's reforms. The remainder of this essay will examine two aspects of this Catholic historical moment, both of them central to the postconciliar dynamic of change in American Catholicism.

## The End of a Subculture

The first of these has to do with the final collapse of the American Catholic subculture, which coincided almost exactly with the Second Vatican Council. That collapse had almost nothing to do with the Council itself—upward mobility and suburbanization had seriously undermined the Catholic subculture before the Council began. Indeed, some historians have questioned whether American Catholics can accurately be described as a subcultural population in the 1950s. But to make this argument one must ignore some crucially important realities. American seminaries were filled to bursting in the 1950s, when new seminaries were opened and existing ones expanded at a rate never previously equaled.[4] Women's religious vocations boomed too. Parochial education remained popular with Catholic parents, even as suburbanization created the expensive burden of building and staffing numerous new schools. Catholic colleges and social service agencies proliferated in these years. Perhaps most important, at least in terms of immediate postconciliar change, compliance with Catholic teaching on birth control appeared to be remarkably widespread. About 70 percent of Catholic women of child-bearing age reported in a 1955 survey that they had never used any means of family limitation other than abstinence or rhythm. (Even those who were not telling the truth are still telling us something important about the Catholic world they inhabited.) Very large families were a hallmark of Catholic life in those distant days; on my own suburban block I remember a family with eight children, one with ten, and one with thirteen. Ours was an affluent suburb, by the by, which is apropos. Fidelity to Catholic teaching on birth control was highest among the best-educated Catholic women, with graduates of Catholic colleges expressing preference for the largest families of all.[5]

Indeed, we can say as a general rule that the Catholics best equipped by reason of education and worldly achievement to flourish outside a subcultural setting were the ones in the 1950s most inclined to champion subcultural values. They took a defiant pride in those aspects of Catholic life and teaching that seemed wrong-headed or even perverse to outsiders—the absolute ban on contraception and remarriage after divorce, the escalating burden of tuition for chronically underresourced schools, the premium placed on submission to authority. Theirs was perhaps less a subculture than a counterculture—a world where holy foolishness was prized and delighted in. To evoke the flavor of this world, let us consider the following letter, written early in 1962 by Father William Sherzer to the chancellor of the Archdiocese of Detroit. The late Father Sherzer, ordained in 1945, was a learned and genuinely scholarly man. Somewhat unusually, given the emphasis placed by devout families on Catholic education for their children, his undergraduate degree came from the University of Michigan. In 1962, Sherzer was a professor of church history at Sacred Heart Seminary in Detroit. Here is what he wrote: "It would be a considerable help to me in my work of teaching history and in my ecumenical contacts with the Protestants if I could have permission to read materials which are on the Index [of Prohibited Books]—largely for dogmatic rather than for moral reasons. [He would have had in mind such things as the works of Luther and Calvin.] Is there any chance of getting such permission? Also, a Catholic M.D. has asked me to act as intermediary in seeking permission to read a book called *The Hunchback of Notre Dame*, in English translation from the French. I do not believe that this person would be endangered in faith or morals by the granting of such permission. Yet there is no other reason behind the petition than the simple wish to read a novel which has somehow engaged [his] interest."[6] Father Sherzer eventually got the permission he sought, though it took an appeal to Rome. The Catholic M.D. did not. The Index was abolished just a few years after this letter, in 1966. One wonders if our dutiful physician had by that time already read Victor Hugo on his own initiative.

For all their deference to authority, highly educated Catholics in the 1950s were aware of, and typically sympathetic to, reforming currents in the Church. Many had participated in Catholic Action, where lay leadership was the norm. Most were partisans of the movement for liturgical reform, the animating logic of which centered on greater lay understanding of and participation in the Mass. They had been schooled, in short, to a sense of ownership in the Church. By the end of the decade, the contradictions inherent in their circumstances had begun to show. One finds the first public murmurings against Catholic teaching on birth control at the end of the 1950s, though the solution almost invariably proposed was not a change in the teaching, still widely assumed infallible, but further research on the rhythm method to make it more effective. One finds public questioning as well with regard to the ideal of a numerous family. Is it really moral to have more children than one can educate through college? Might the emotional development of children be neglected when births come too frequently?[7] Historians are also beginning to document the changing liturgical tastes of the later 1950s, when novenas and such public displays of Catholic ritual otherness as Holy Hours in local sports stadiums suddenly began drawing fewer participants.[8] And perhaps most tellingly, mission preachers from various religious orders were complaining by then that Catholics were losing their tolerance for graphic sermons on hell.[9] We should also note a significant development in the nation's seminaries. In the late 1950s, attrition from those seminaries began to rise in every region of the country, including attrition in the final stages of preparation for the priesthood.[10]

Many Catholic laity thus entered the years of the Council with curiously divided hearts and minds. They were simultaneously partisans of reform and deeply invested in a particularly demanding vision of Catholic tradition. One could say something similar of many young priests, who even at the Council's opening were restive with regard to the peculiar strictures of their situation—the waits of twenty years and more to become a pastor, the concomitant inability to use one's skills and initiative to the full—but not yet ready to question their status as men set apart or the discipline of mandatory celibacy. As it became increasingly clear that the Council was moving in unexpectedly progressive directions, many laity and younger clergy responded with a kind of euphoria—an exhilaration that testifies to the internal conflicts that growing numbers were experiencing. A reform-minded Council held out the prospect of a less tightly bounded and less burdened Catholic existence—something for which there was genuine hunger by the early 1960s. Euphoria of this sort necessarily breeds impatience. Impatience with the inevitably slow nature of ecclesial reform bred resentment, which occasionally soured into bitterness. And resentment gave rise, with growing frequency, to intemperate rhetoric. Thus a Council where a premium had been placed on mutually respectful dialogue gave way to an increasingly nasty family feud over the nature of authority in the Church.

## Change Driven from Below

Birth control was the single most potent driver of this conflict, simply because it affected so many Catholics in such intimate and life-altering fashion. With birth control, we have a near-perfect example of the change dynamic that evolved in the American Church in the wake of Vatican II. Change with regard to birth control began at the grass roots. More and more Catholics began to make use of forbidden modes of family limitation, a trend that dates from the later 1950s. And more and more Catholics were willing to challenge the teaching, citing not just its near-insuperable difficulty but calling into question its fundamental morality. Could a teaching so destructive of marital happiness really reflect the will of God? Some articulated their discontent publicly. Lay-authored articles on the question of birth control, nearly all of them critical of Church teaching, proliferated in 1964 and after. Many more laity spoke frankly to their priests, growing numbers of whom began in consequence to alter their practice as confessors. It was not at all difficult, by 1966, to find a priest who would advise you to follow your conscience with regard to the use of birth control, which more and more Catholics were in fact doing.[11]

Theologians joined the conversation too, largely in response to the groundswell of lay opposition. By 1967, most of the nation's leading moral theologians had become critics of the teaching, which effectively rendered its status doubtful, at least in the eyes of many clergy. A doubtful law does not bind, as every seminarian knew. His penitents "commonly engage in long arguments in the Confessional stating that different priests give contradictory answers and do not agree with each other," as a Baltimore priest recounted his recent experiences as a confessor in 1966.[12] Even bishops were occasionally converted by means of lay testimony, as we see in the final report of the Papal Commission on Population, Births, and the Family—that now-forgotten 1966 document that advised Pope Paul VI to allow married couples to make their own prayerful decisions about family planning. If the pope rejected their advice, as he famously did in *Humanae Vitae*, he was unable to stop or even slow the grassroots movement toward reform. By the mid-1970s, Catholic contraceptive use in the United States was indistinguishable from that of other Americans, once one adjusted for education and income, save that Catholics were still less likely than other Americans to have recourse to sterilization—a distinction that ultimately disappeared, as well. As for American priests, they seldom broached the subject after 1968, ceding this particular moral ground to the private choices of the laity.

The same change dynamic becomes evident in other areas too. Let us consider reform of the liturgy. As the American bishops envisioned it, reform would proceed—under episcopal direction—by means of what Detroit's Cardinal John Dearden called "controlled experimentation." The national Bishops' Conference, in other words, would coordinate the cautious phasing in of new ritual practices, with parishes designated in certain dioceses as the authorized sites for carefully monitored liturgical experiments. What actually happened differed quite markedly. Nearly all

Archbishop Dearden with members of the Grail in Detroit, 1959. An international Catholic women's movement and prime exemplar of Catholic Action, the Grail was especially known in the 1940s and 1950s for its commitment to liturgical renewal. Its Detroit chapter had a particular interest in what used to be called the Negro Apostolate. (Archives of the Archdiocese of Detroit)

liturgical innovations of the later 1960s and the early 1970s—communion under both species at most Masses, communion in the hand, lay ministers of the Eucharist, altar girls—began as unauthorized practice in avowedly progressive parishes. Episcopal approval followed later, often after the practice in question had begun to be widely embraced. "It is generally felt that the Bishops are not offering leadership in the liturgical area," in the opinion of a Midwestern liturgist in 1969. "To many of the priests it seems they are always reacting and solidifying by law what has been common practice of the church for some time."[13]

To what extent did the laity drive liturgical innovation? Only a small proportion of laypeople in the immediate post-Council years could be described a liturgically avant-garde—perhaps 10 percent in a typical suburban parish, according to the liturgist just quoted.[14] Such advanced laypersons, however, proved essential support to those priests—mostly young—who wanted to experiment with liturgy, something they could not do in the absence of a congregation. Much of the bolder experimentation, moreover, took place at Masses said in private homes, where liturgical creativity had completely free rein. Cardinal Dearden spoke with real dismay in 1968 of the "literally bizarre departures from established procedures" that had come to his attention.[15] In these respects, reform was at least partly lay-driven. It was certainly the laity who transformed the place of confession in Catholic life, simply by staying away from the sacrament. Frequent confession—monthly or even weekly—had been a hallmark of the preconciliar Church in the United States. By the early 1970s, growing numbers of Catholics confessed only once a year—the minimum required by Canon Law—and some abandoned the practice entirely.[16] Let us also note one additional change in liturgical behavior, minor but indisputably lay-driven: at some point in the later 1960s, Catholic women stopped covering their heads in church, to the distress of many older priests.

Remarriage after divorce represents the final area where grassroots pressures in the wake of the Council led to major institutional change. As any Catholic at the time of the Council could have told you, marriage was indissoluble. A Catholic might obtain a civil divorce, but no divorced Catholic—indeed, no divorced person—was canonically free to marry again as long as his or her former spouse was still alive. One could certainly marry civilly or in a Protestant ceremony. But in the eyes of the Catholic Church, those who did—and here we have reference to Catholics and non-Catholics alike—were living in mortal sin, literally committing adultery on a daily basis. What about getting the marriage annulled, today's young Catholic might ask. Even after the Council, the grounds for annulment proved so stringent and the procedure for obtaining an annulment so slow and expensive that very few Catholics attempted it. Most American Catholics at the time of the Council regarded Church teaching on marriage with ambivalence. Insofar as the teaching endorsed permanence as the marital ideal, it met acceptance in principle. But many Catholics were also troubled by the suffering it caused, particularly with the divorce rate soaring after the mid-1960s.

No one has yet closely studied the process by which the American church became the principal grantor of annulments in the world. (About 70 percent of Catholic annulments granted worldwide are issued in the United States.)[17] But grassroots pressure was a key factor. Even in the later 1960s, divorced Catholics asked their priests about the possibility of remarrying in the Church—something they had never done before, simply because it would have been pointless. Some of those priests began to opt for what was called the "pastoral solution in the internal forum," which means that a priest agrees to marry couples whose disposition and circumstances seem to warrant it and encourages them to receive the Eucharist as validly married Catholics. How could they do otherwise, many such priests asked, since they believed that priests who left the active ministry had the right to be speedily dispensed from the vow of celibacy? Bishops were naturally troubled by what they saw as the issuance of bootleg annulments; some responded by liberalizing their diocesan annulment procedures to make them more generous and "user-friendly." The process of liberalization proceeded more slowly than many clergy would have liked, given the pastoral difficulties posed by divorced Catholics, and varied from one diocese to the next. But proceed it did. American dioceses granted a total of 368 annulments in 1968. Between 1984 and 1994 in the United States, an average of 58,000 annulments were granted annually.[18]

Those hyperactive marriage tribunals, which some have called veritable annulment mills, point to the complexities, and indeed the ironies, of postconciliar reform. A link exists to the Council itself: the Council Fathers spoke of marriage as a covenant and an intimate relationship, which permitted canonists to argue that immature persons might lack the ability to contract a sacramental union. Hence the greatly expanded grounds for annulment. As we have seen, the process of reform was driven by change at the grass roots—by a laity now vulnerable to the realities of a divorce-prone culture but no longer willing to suffer life-long as a consequence of Catholic legalism; by a clergy who had its own reasons to oppose legalism and top-down authority. As with birth control, the institutional Church kept a traditional teaching formally intact—"on the books," as it were—even as practice and popular understanding changed. Not surprisingly, this fostered a certain cynicism in the Catholic ranks. Between 80 and 90 percent of annulment petitions filed in the United States prove successful. And yet most divorced Catholics do not seek annulments, typically opting to remarry before someone other than a priest. Many Catholics today are critical of the annulment process, regarding it as dishonest, invasive of privacy, and even cruel.[19] So we have enormous change, on the one hand, but discontent and a degree of bitterness too—along with a climate that prevents frank discussion of what Christian marriage can and should look like in the world we inhabit. None of this has much to do with what the Council Fathers hoped for.

## Catholics and Race

A collapsing Catholic subculture, then, magnified the impact of conciliar reforms in the United States. You may recall that this was the first of two topics I wanted to address as significant aspects of the historical circumstances in which American Catholics received the Council's reforms. I would now like to turn to the second—quite different from the first but no less important. What I have in mind is the politics of race in the urban North, where the vast majority of the nation's Catholics lived. John McGreevy has written brilliantly on this subject in *Parish Boundaries*.[20] But his insights have not yet been adequately incorporated into accounts of the post-Council years, perhaps because the subject does not fit neatly into the customary categories of "church history." Tensions over race, however, did far more to polarize Catholics after the Council than did any purely ecclesial reforms, especially but not exclusively in the nation's big cities.

My recent research has principally focused on the Archdiocese of Detroit. No better place exists in which to examine the Catholic encounter with race and civil rights activism. Like other industrial cities, Detroit sustained a massive in-migration of Southern blacks in the 1940s and 1950s, which coincided with an increasing outflow of whites to the suburbs. The city was about 16 percent African American in 1950, a figure that rose to 30 percent just ten years later; it became a black-majority city in the early 1970s. Because Detroit was a high-wage city, average income among the city's blacks in the 1950s and 1960s was the highest in the nation. The local auto industry, however, had already gone into decline, as the Big Three built their new plants mostly outside southeastern Michigan and the smaller producers who had survived the Depression went out of business. Both Hudson and Packard closed massive production facilities in Detroit in the mid-1950s. A gradually slowing local economy meant a growing population of chronically unemployed or underemployed workers, many of them young and black. That street crime was rising by the early 1960s will hardly come as a surprise.

Detroit's white population in the 1950s and 1960s was heavily Catholic, as was the local political elite. The city, with 128 parishes, was honeycombed with Catholic churches and schools. But less than 3 percent of Detroit's African American population was Catholic, which presented an obvious problem to Detroit's new archbishop, John Francis Dearden, when he arrived in 1959. What to do about those vast parish plants in the many center-city neighborhoods rapidly transitioning from white to black? Dearden's initial interest in the politics of race appears to have

Participants in a 1965 Human Dignity conference in Detroit,
sponsored by the Archbishop's Commission on Human Relations.
(Archives of the Archdiocese of Detroit)

stemmed primarily from this concern, since he knew very little, at this juncture, about the particulars of black life in Detroit. When he established the Archbishop's Commission on Human Relations in 1960, its programming aimed both at stimulating conversions among African Americans—successors, it was devoutly hoped, to departing white Catholics in the center-city parishes—as well as at encouraging whites to stay in their neighborhoods and facilitate peaceful integration.

Archbishop—later Cardinal—John Dearden is invariably described by his contemporaries as a man who was transformed by the Second Vatican Council. Known as "Iron John" in his previous assignment as bishop of Pittsburgh, he arrived in Detroit with a reputation for playing strictly by the rules. At the Council, however, he emerged as a quiet force in the reform-minded majority, playing an especially significant role in the drafting of the 1965 Pastoral on the Church in the Modern World, or *Gaudium et Spes*. (He chaired the subcommittee responsible for drafting the chapter on the potentially explosive topic of marriage and the family.) After the close of the Council, he became a force for reform in his role as chairman, from 1966 until 1971, of the National Council of Catholic Bishops, and certainly in his own archdiocese, where he showed legendary patience with the more radical of his clergy. Detroit was widely regarded in the post-Council years as the most progressive of the nation's large urban dioceses, both for the climate of freedom that prevailed there and for the boldness of the racial initiatives undertaken by the Dearden chancery.

Although Dearden often justified those racial initiatives by invoking the Council documents, especially *Gaudium et Spes*, local circumstances in good part shaped his evolving views on race. Despite an innately moderate temperament, he was perceptibly radicalized by the terrible rioting that killed more than forty people in Detroit in July 1967. His post-riot radicalism created deep divisions in the archdiocese. For a significant portion of his flock, disproportionately but not exclusively working-class, Dearden's newly proactive stance on race constituted a kind of betrayal. In their view, he had turned his back on a tradition of Catholic leadership by which the Church protected the Catholic tribe and its fierce ethos of localism. (The pro-union stance of Dearden's predecessor, who seldom mentioned race, was regarded by many of his critics as the kind of social Catholicism they favored.) "They still accept the old values and they perceive the Cardinal as the enemy," Father Thomas Hinsberg told Dearden with regard to the many local Catholics whom he frankly regarded as racists.[21] For others, often but not invariably highly educated and affluent, their archbishop's radicalism was a source of pride and an affirmation of the Catholic universalism they associated with the Council.

Dearden spoke about race in guarded terms in the early 1960s and trod carefully for a time thereafter. He endorsed the 1964 Civil Rights Act and permitted his priests to go to Selma, but he refrained from endorsing open housing legislation in Detroit, where it faced strong opposition from Catholic voters.[22] The most important initiative of these years was something called Project Commitment, which was under the direction of the Archbishop's Commission on Human Relations and very much shaped by the activist priests who ran it. The roots of the program date to 1961, when so-called leadership training sessions were held in selected city and suburban parishes with the aim of creating within the archdiocese a corps of lay leaders who could advocate effectively for the peaceful integration of their neighborhoods. (Detroit had a history of violent white resistance to expansion of the historically black areas of settlement, so such leaders were definitely needed.)[23] After a pilot program in 1965, Project Commitment got under way in 1966. It too involved leadership training, but on a far more ambitious scale. The goal was to have a Human Relations Committee in every parish, working to change local attitudes on race, discouraging panic selling when blacks first moved in, welcoming black Catholics to the parish, and overseeing the integration of the parish school. Several thousand Detroit-area Catholics underwent Project Commitment training in what was undoubtedly the most far-reaching racial initiative undertaken by any Catholic diocese in the country.

Project Commitment proceeded in the context of rapid racial change in the city. Many of the affected neighborhoods were heavily Catholic, where anxieties ran high. Did Dearden understand or care about the costs that swift racial change exacted from whites? Many Catholics came to doubt it, as did some of their priests. Catholics like these were deeply fearful of the expanding black population; regarding themselves as victims, they vehemently denied the frequent charge of racism. "I, as a white, have less rights here in my home-town than any field negro recently transplanted here from the fields of Alabama," in the all-too-typical words of an irate Detroiter, writing from what she described as a newly integrated and crime-plagued neighborhood.[24] Working-class Catholics often saved in the form of home ownership, which helps to explain their obsessive worries about declining property values. These were inevitable, residents widely believed, in the event of neighborhood integration. Either one sold immediately and took a loss or stayed until life became intolerable, by which time the value of one's property would have plummeted even further. And life would indeed become intolerable, according to the prevailing logic, since the presence of blacks would mean rising street crime and perhaps, in the context of a dwindling Catholic population, the eventual closure of the parish school.

Detroit's recent history, moreover, strongly suggested that neighborhoods in transition eventually resegregated—a reality that Dearden's racial initiatives simply could not address. Even when some whites remained, new white families did not move in. "This does not help the colored people achieve integration in housing," as a veteran of Project Commitment noted, when his own neighborhood was rapidly losing its remaining white residents, "and it does leave the white people remaining in the city in an uncertain position as the area becomes a new extension of the so-called colored 'ghetto.'"[25] The archives of the archdiocese contain numerous angry letters raging against these perceived grim alternatives. Those letters contain their share and more of overt racism, some it of crude. But there is pathos too. If the writers were implicated in the historical processes currently upending their lives, they frequently did

St. Cecilia's church, located in one of the many Detroit neighborhoods that transitioned in the 1960s from all white to nearly all black, flourished for a time thereafter as a center of African American Catholicism. Parishioner DeVon Cunningham, shown here, painted an apse mural in the church in 1968 featuring a black Christ surrounded by multiethnic angels. (Archives of the Archdiocese of Detroit)

not understand them. And as more than one pointed out, much of the progressive Catholic leadership locally, including Dearden himself, lived either in all-white neighborhoods on the fringes of the city or in its segregated suburbs.

As noted, the civil disorders of July 1967 pushed Dearden toward a more proactive stance. Shortly thereafter, he testified in favor of an open housing ordinance before the Detroit City Council. He endorsed the findings of the Kerner Commission on the causes of urban rioting and dispatched a specially trained corps of priests to do the same in pulpits throughout the archdiocese. In Dearden's view, the Kerner Commission had been right to attribute recent urban violence to white racism, although whites themselves tended to deny this. "We cannot leave [our people] contentedly in this state," he told his priests. "Whether they like it or not they must hear it."[26] Most controversially, he announced that nearly all the money collected in 1968 for the Archdiocesan Development Fund, which had previously been directed toward support and expansion of local Catholic institutions, would be devoted to projects in Detroit's poor black neighborhoods, some of them under non-Catholic auspices. In conjunction with this announcement, Dearden pledged his support for inner-city Catholic schools, most of which now enrolled numerous black students, many of them non-Catholic. He stuck to this commitment in subsequent years, even after financial pressures forced the closure of scores of parochial schools throughout the archdiocese. When the prospect of city-suburban busing loomed in metro Detroit in the early 1970s, Dearden forbade his priests to accept pupils in their schools whose Catholic parents apparently sought to evade the busing order, even when enhanced enrollment might have saved the school in question.

Dearden's newly proactive stance on race put him at odds with many Catholics locally. Contributions to the Archdiocesan Development Fund fell sharply in 1968 and remained at low ebb for some years thereafter. Tensions increased even more when the Dearden chancery ordered the closure of dozens of parish schools after Michigan voters in 1970 approved a ballot measure prohibiting state assistance to non-public education. Many of the affected schools were in deep financial trouble, compelled as they had recently been to hire large numbers of lay teachers whose salaries were far greater than those traditionally paid to women religious. But because of Dearden's highly public commitment to subsidize at least some of Detroit's center-city schools, many local Catholics believed that their own schools had fallen victim to their now cardinal archbishop's civil rights agenda. "Very many . . . are blaming the Archbishop for deliberately closing our schools for 'civil rights' or 'racial' purposes, feeling that the schools could have somehow stayed open if only he had kept out of things," according to a layman from suburban Detroit. "We have all heard these views in our office, at parties, at parish affairs and on the street."[27]

What has this dispiriting state of affairs to do with the Second Vatican Council? Interestingly, people on both sides of the divide invoked the Council in their defense. Those hostile to Dearden's racial initiatives championed the rights of the laity against a heavy-handed chancery, stoking a suspicion of ecclesial authority that would prove long lasting. Invoking the Council's declaration on religious liberty with specific refer- ence to local school closings, one indignant correspondent charged that Dearden had violated parents' fundamental right to choose "the kind of religious education their children are to receive." Since the state permitted the existence of non-public schools, "we do not accept the Church's right to deprive us of this freedom."[28] Dearden's supporters, by contrast, spoke in terms of a Church open to the world, prioritizing the needs of the poor over the claims of fellow Catholics. Such, in their view, was the principal message of the Council documents.

Dearden's critics, as we have seen, believed him guilty of communal betrayal, though their worldview gradually evolved toward a kind of ecu- menism, which involved a growing sense of kinship with non-Catholics who placed a high priority on family and conventional gender roles. This sensibility came to fruition in the antiabortion movement of the 1970s. Catholic progressives, for their part, felt increasingly repelled by anything that hinted at tribalism. By the mid-1960s, indeed, some were embarrassed by the chancery's encouragement of evangelization in the black commu- nity, fearing that it smacked of Catholic triumphalism and implied disre- spect for black culture. Did Catholics not have much to learn from black civil rights activists, with roots typically in the black Protestant churches? Had they not modeled virtue in a way few Catholics could equal? Not sur- prisingly, evangelization was something of an afterthought in diocesan programming by the later 1960s.

I do not claim that Dearden's sometimes-racist opponents correctly interpreted the Council, which in any event never challenged the right of a bishop to govern his diocese as he saw fit. I do, however, think the Coun- cil made it easier for such people to speak a language of rights with regard to Church authority. In the final analysis, racial progressives emerged as the Council's natural heirs—but their experiences also most clearly deline- ate the hazards attendant on the Council's much-admired "opening to the world." Let me close with some instructive vignettes from a 1966 experiment in Detroit called Project Community. Project Community brought together some thirty nuns from several different religious orders for a summer of "being present" in one of Detroit's poorest neighborhoods, once mostly Polish and now almost entirely African American. Using a local community center as their base, the sisters visited homes, offered assistance where they could, and simply got to know the locals. According to their journals, the experience was transformative. They learned a freer use of the body, as local children demanded hugs and kisses. By opening up their place of residence to those in need, they experienced a less restrictive common life. As one sister explained, "We have staying with us, Lisa, a young woman from the Women's Correction Center. She really is a good girl—and her staying with us is as good for us as it is for her. *So much of our traditional 'convent mentality' is breaking down, thank God!*"[29]

The sisters also experimented with the liturgy, encouraged in this regard by a priest who pointed out that while he was bound by liturgical rules, lay people—and nuns are such—were not. So they composed their own bidding prayers, sang folk hymns at Mass, encouraged their celebrants to engage in dialogue homilies, and organized a communal penance service. Perhaps most important, they lived for the first time in their lives surrounded by non-Catholics, whose spiritual resources they came to admire. Project Community staged a farewell gathering in August for a group of older neighborhood residents to whom many of the sisters had become attached. Toward the end of the afternoon, one Louise Finch asked if she might say a few words, since she had to leave soon to preach at a local church. Here is how Sister Juliana remembers the moment: "If only everyone could have heard the warm, loving, grateful words spoken in rich tones by this 250–300 pound woman in [a] long flowing, yellowed-white satin preaching robe. She spoke of the love she has for the Sisters who have been present these weeks and who have been so lovingly helpful to all the neighbors. She hopes we'll be back soon. And then she commented on the need for all of us Christians to love one another in the Spirit of Christ. . . . A Sister who just came home from Collegeville theology studies and stopped in for a visit said, 'This woman *knows* St. Paul's doctrine on love!'"[30]

I do not know what happened next to the veterans of Project Community. But I doubt that they found it easy to submit to the still-restrictive discipline of the convents they returned to or to accept without question the authority structures of a Church in which women could not yet even serve as lectors at Mass.[31] For me, these sisters embody the intense ambiguities of the postconciliar years. The reforms of the Council, I think they would have said, had made it possible for them to be more authentic Christians, and with almost bewildering speed. (Project Community took place only six months after the close of the Council.) What more appropriate outcome for a Council that had issued a universal call to holiness? But the sisters' new experience of Christian witness, however gratifying, probably made it harder for these admirable women to be Roman Catholics. Welcome to the world, we might say in response, where ambiguity abounds.

NOTES

1. O'Malley, *What Happened At Vatican II*, 306.

2. Sermon outline for the 24th Sunday after Pentecost, 17 Nov. 1963. Detroit, Mich., Archives of the Archdiocese of Detroit, Worship Department, Box 2, Folder Sermon Outlines, 1959–1966.

3. Greeley, *The American Catholic*, 56–57.

4. There were 388 Catholic seminaries in the United States in 1950, and 525 a decade later. In this same period, the number of seminarians grew from about 26,000 to almost 40,000. O'Brien, *The Renewal of American Catholicism*, 139.

5. On this subject see Tentler, *Catholics and Contraception*, especially 133–36.

6. Fr. William Sherzer to Msgr. Bernard Kearns, 5 March 1962. Detroit, Mich., Archives of the Archdiocese of Detroit Worship Department, Box 1, Folder Liturgical Commission, 1959–1963.

7. Tentler, *Catholics and Contraception*, 199–203.

8. Greeley, "Popular Devotions"; Tentler, *Seasons of Grace*, 408–13; Kelly, *The Transformation of American Catholicism*, especially 20–59; McCartin, *Prayers of the Faithful*, 106–8.

9. Tentler, *Catholics and Contraception*, 159–61.

10. Cuyler, "Perseverance Trends in the Seminary," documents both the rise in attrition and the previously mentioned uptick in seminary enrollments in the early 1960s.

11. Tentler, *Catholics and Contraception*, 210–32, 242–47.

12. N.N. to Cardinal Lawrence Shehan, 20 May 1966. Baltimore, Md., Archives of the Archdiocese of Baltimore, Lawrence Shehan Papers.

13. Fr. Patrick Cooney to Bishop Thomas Gumbleton, 9 April 1969. Detroit, Mich., Archives of the Archdiocese of Detroit, Worship Department, Box 1, Folder Gumbleton (Vicar for Parishes), 1969–1971.

14. Fr. Patrick Cooney to Bishop Thomas Gumbleton, 30 March 1970. Detroit, Mich., Archives of the Archdiocese of Detroit, Worship Department, Box 1, Folder Gumbleton (Vicar for Parishes), 1969–1971.

15. "Archbishop's Meeting with Priests," typescript, 14 March 1968. Detroit, Mich., Archives of the Archdiocese of Detroit, Dearden Papers, Box 23 [temporary cataloguing], not yet in folder.

16. O'Toole, "In the Court of Conscience," 168–71; see also Saldahna, "American Catholics—Ten Years Later," 15.

17. Hegy and Martos, *Catholic Divorce*, 2.

18. Hegy, "Catholic Divorce, Annulments, and Deception," in Hegy and Martos, *Catholic Divorce*, 11.

19. Ibid., 11, 21; see also Hegy and Martos, *Catholic Divorce*, 2.

20. McGreevy, *Parish Boundaries*.

21. Fr. Thomas F. Hinsberg to Dearden, 27 Nov. 1970. Notre Dame, Ind., Archives of the University of Notre Dame, Thomas Gumbleton Papers [CGUM], Box 48, Folder 9.

22. The archdiocesan newspaper, closely linked to the chancery, did editorialize in support of open occupancy.

23. See Sugrue, *The Origins of the Urban Crisis*, 179–258.

24. "Sad Catholic Detroiter" to Dearden, 25 June 1963. Detroit, Mich., Archives of the Archdiocese of Detroit, Archbishop's Commission on Human Relations Collection, Box 7, Folder 18.

25. John E. Tobin to Dearden, 17 Feb. 1966. Detroit, Mich., Archives of the Archdiocese of Detroit, Archbishop's Commission on Human Relations Collection, Box 6, Folder 12.

26 Archbishop John Dearden, "Talk to Clergy re: Kerner Report," undated typescript but 14 March 1968. Detroit, Mich., Archives of the Archdiocese of Detroit, Dearden Papers, Box 23 [temporary cataloguing], not yet in folder.

27. Ed Rooney, "Some Thoughts on the School Closings," undated but 1971, prepared for the parish council of St. Paul's, Grosse Pointe. Detroit, Mich., Archives of the Archdiocese of Detroit, Dearden Papers, Box 13, Folder School Closings.

28. Anonymous to Dearden, undated but late 1970 or early 1971. Notre Dame, Ind., Archives of the University of Notre Dame, CGUM, Box 48, Folder 11.

29. Sister Maria Goretti, SNDdeN, "Report on Project Blecki," 3 Aug. 1966. Detroit, Mich., Archives of the Archdiocese of Detroit, Archbishop's Commission on Human Relations, Box 2, Folder 28; emphasis in original. Blecki was the name of the local community center.

30. "Summary of Project Community," no author given but almost certainly Glenmary Sister Juliana, undated but August 1966. Detroit, Mich., Archives of the Archdiocese of Detroit, Archbishop's Commission on Human Relations, Box 2, Folder 28.

31. When the revised English-Latin Sacramentary was published in 1966, it read: "The Conference of Bishops has given permission that, when a qualified man is not available, a woman may proclaim the readings prior to the gospel, while standing outside the sanctuary." Hardly a giant step forward! See Catholic Church, *English—Latin Sacramentary for the USA*, 60.

## 3

# THE EXERCISE OF ECCLESIAL AUTHORITY IN LIGHT OF VATICAN II

*Catherine E. Clifford*

According to Catholic teaching, an ecumenical council represents a privileged moment, the most concentrated and comprehensive exercise of doctrinal authority and decision making in the life of the Church.[1] Councils are perhaps the most effective way that Christians have found to discern the mind of the whole church. An ecumenical council constitutes a concentrated expression of the dynamic set of relationships that should characterize our living together as church at all times. As a gathering of the bishops who preside over all local churches, a council's ecumenicity is founded on the conviction that the Gospel has been entrusted to the whole church, and comes from this representative character: the conciliar assembly represents and speaks to the church in its entirety. Because it expresses the faith of the whole church, an ecumenical council constitutes the most authoritative teaching body in the Church. To determine what Vatican II has to say about the exercise of ecclesial authority and decision making in the Church, I propose a reflection based on the history of the Council itself. As I hope to show, the conflict and tensions experienced within the Council remain very much alive today. They continue to influence the interpretation of the Council and its teaching. Lastly, they reveal some of the most important issues that have yet to be faced if other Christians are ever to consider entering concretely into unity with the Catholic Church.[2]

## Authority as Service

All authority in the Church has its source in Christ. The New Testament uses the term *exousia* to denote this authority that comes from God alone. It has no equivalent in the English language, although its etymology suggests that it refers to a power or force that derives from the nature of the person acting, from a consonance of word and deed. Saint Paul writes in the Letter to the Romans that "there is no authority except from

God" (Romans 13:1; cf. John 19:11). All ecclesial authority derives from this divine source. The authority of Jesus is evident in the consonance of his life and teaching (Luke 4:32; Matthew 7:29), and manifested in acts of forgiveness and healing (Mark 2:10; Luke 5:24; Mark 3:15; cf. Matthew 28:18; John 17:2). By this same authority, Jesus freely lays down his life for us (John 10:18; cf. Mark 10:44–45).

The example of Christ signifies that all genuine authority is service, a liberating force intended for the benefit of others, to assist them on the path toward the fullness of life. The term *exousia* is used in the Second Letter to the Corinthians to denote the authority that Paul received from the Lord for the building up of the Christian community (2 Corinthians 10:8, 13:10). Christ is the source and the model of all authority in the Church, a community that by its nature is called to be of service to the entire human community. The Christological grounding of ecclesial authority becomes apparent in Vatican II's insistence on authority or hierarchy as service,[3] as well as in its affirmation that every exercise of the pastoral teaching office lies not above, but serves the Word of God revealed in Christ and handed on through the Scriptures.[4]

The Second Vatican Council proved a significant moment in the history of the Catholic Church for its recovery of an understanding of authority as service. At the risk of oversimplifying, one can detect in the language and style of engagement that characterizes the Council's teaching a return to a more ancient model or conception of authority and its exercise. Rooted in the witness of scripture and tradition, it is marked by a rediscovery of the basic equality and dignity of all baptized Christians, of an understanding of the Church as a communion of diverse local churches. This rediscovery brought about a return to understanding the collegial nature of the episcopal office. More broadly, the Second Vatican Council marks a definitive shift away from a pyramidal, monarchical conception of the Church—shaped by centuries of history in which the Western church evolved according to a Constantinian fusion of church and state marked by competing temporal and spiritual powers, which the Benedictine theologian Ghislain Lafont has called the "Gregorian form"[5] of the Church—and a return to the notion of the Church as a communion, which had prevailed throughout the first millennium of Christianity.[6] It might be further characterized as a shift from a model of "power over" and obediential compliance to authority as service and shared obedience in a common engagement for the discernment of the Gospel.

We can locate a fundamental key to understanding this shift in both the form and the exercise of authority by the Second Vatican Council itself, especially as reflected in the sixteen documents. These are remarkable for both their massive volume and their dialogical style. When compared to the volume of texts represented by the twenty preceding ecumenical councils, the documents of Vatican II account for almost one third of all writings from ecumenical councils, or almost half the number of pages produced by the previous twenty. The length of these texts derives from the Council's distinctive style of teaching. The Jesuit historian John O'Malley has suggested that if we are to arrive at an adequate understanding of the Council and it its documents, we must appreciate the extent to which its mode of teaching and in its conception of the life and mission of the Church deliberately inscribed the dynamics of dialogical engagement.[7] It is instructive to turn to the experience of the Council itself to see how the bishops of Vatican II came to adopt this distinctive form in the exercise of their pastoral teaching office.

## Council: An Experience of Dialogue

The 2,600 bishops who gathered in Rome during four sessions that met each fall from 1962 to 1965 were themselves deeply marked by the experience of collegial dialogue and became convinced of its importance for the form and content of the Council's teaching. They experienced a deepening awareness of the Church as a communion of all the baptized, whose inner vitality and outreach rely on the synergetic cooperation of all as we place our gifts at the service of God's Spirit.

Bishops gathered in council must attend to the voice of all the faithful to discern the living faith of the Church. They weigh the contributions of theologians and other experts, and consider the merits of various approaches and formulations of doctrine. In the context of conciliar debate, they learn from the experience of fellow bishops about the living faith of the Church as experienced in other regions of the world, and in different ecclesial traditions. The bishops of the Latin Church at Vatican II learned greatly from their fellow bishops of the twenty-two Eastern Catholic Churches. Karl Rahner has famously argued that the Second Vatican Council began a process whereby the Catholic Church became aware of itself as truly a "world church" for the first time in history.[8] Indigenous bishops from Asia, Africa, and Latin America managed to voice the pastoral needs of Catholic Christians in diverse non-European contexts, and to bring the living faith of these communities to bear on the witness of the entire church. Their lived experience of dialogue across cultures contributed to a deeper awareness of the Church as a diversity in communion.

The historian Giuseppe Alberigo has written that by the end of the first session of the Council, "the bishops and their 'experts' with them gained an almost totally new awareness of their concrete and common general responsibilities for the universal church."[9] More than one council father has said to me, "I learned what it means to be a bishop at the council." During the years surrounding the Council, the bishops experienced for themselves the necessity and value of dialogue with the faithful of their local churches. Many undertook extensive consultations with the clergy, laity, and religious of their diocese. From the opening days of the Council a handful of lay auditors were present. The French philosopher Jean Guitton, a personal friend of Paul VI, was invited to address the Council on Christian unity near the end of the second session.[10] Another layman, Patrick Keegan, the English president of the World Movement of Christian Workers and a member of the Permanent Committee of the International Congress for the Apostolate of the Laity, presented the Decree on the Apostolate of Laity, *Apostolicam Actuositatem*, to the Council Fathers during the third session.[11] The number of auditors expanded considerably in the third and fourth sessions, in the fall of 1964 and 1965, respectively, to include twenty-three women, lay and religious.[12] While no woman addressed the bishops *in aula*, a good number took an active part in the work of the subcommissions drafting the Decree on the Apostolate of the Laity, and the Pastoral Constitution on the Church in the Modern World.

Finally, the deliberations of the Second Vatican Council are deeply marked by the presence and the regular exchanges that took place between the bishops and the 167 official observers and 22 guests from other Christian churches.[13] Next to the renewal of the Catholic Church, the quest for Christian unity ranged among the Council's most important goals. The Secretariat for Christian Unity, established by Pope John XXIII on the eve of the Council to keep this goal before the Council Fathers in all of its deliberations, organized weekly meetings with the observers where they could make their views known concerning the draft documents. The bishops and the various drafting committees frequently took up these concerns as they proposed amendments and asked for improvements to the schemata.

Recalling his conciliar experience, the Methodist observer Albert Outler writes, "The only significant part of the business of the council that was closed to us were the commission meetings—and even here, as the council wore on, we learned how to get reliable reports of their progress, and how to convey *our* concerns to them. In all these ways and more, the observers constituted a presence in the council that was a dynamic factor in the process."[14] In fact, it was not unusual, as the Council wore on, to discover that the bishops on the Council floor repeated in their interventions points originally raised by the observers. John Moorman, the head of the Council's Anglican delegation, writes of how the Lutheran observer Kristen Skydsgaard criticized the draft document of the Church at one of the weekly meetings organized for the observers. Less than a week later, another observer said to him as they entered St. Peter's Basilica for a general congregation of the Council, "Do you remember Skydsgaard's speech at the meeting last week? . . . Well you're going to hear it again this morning. Cardinal Meyer has heard about it and is going to make the same points."[15]

## John XXIII on the Purpose of the Council and the Form of Its Teaching

In the period leading up to the official opening of the Council on October 11, 1962, it is fair to say that there were competing visions of what a council ought to be, and of how the Church should carry forth its mission in the modern world. Gérard Philips, the assistant secretary of the Doctrinal Commission, aptly described these two broad tendencies in an article published in early 1963, during the first intersession, much to the consternation of the conservative minority.[16] While a desire to preserve the traditional expression of faith motivated the first tendency, a second was more concerned to communicate the message of faith to contemporaries. These two perspectives, reflecting competing ecclesiologies, carried within them differing views of the exercise of ecclesial authority, and in particular of the pastoral teaching office of the bishops, including the Bishop of Rome.

There had been twenty ecumenical councils in the history of the Catholic Church. While a number of these were concerned—not unlike Vatican II—with reform and with attempts to restore church unity, many constituted primarily legislative events that produced declarations of censure and condemnations of doctrinal error. The texts they produced above all wished to "to correct deviations from received teaching and practice."[17] Many—those belonging to the first tendency—expected much the same stance from the Second Vatican Council. It is perhaps not surprising, then, that most of the draft texts brought before the bishops by the Preparatory Commission for their deliberation had been written largely in this vein. Yet the conciliar majority, who welcomed the guiding vision of Pope John XXIII, was more concerned with the challenge of proclaiming the Gospel in a manner that would engage contemporary society and culture.

In his official convocation of the Second Vatican Council, Pope John invited the bishops to embrace what we now recognize as a distinctive style of teaching that sets the Second Vatican Council apart from previous councils. He insisted that the changing circumstances of the world necessitated an updating (*aggiornamento*) of the Church. "Humanity is at the threshold of a new age," he said, and the Church should be concerned to bring the "perennial life-giving energies of the Gospel to the modern world."[18] While the Catholic Church had long held a fearful stance toward modernity, Pope John preferred to look to the "signs of the times" for reasons to hope for the future of the Church and of humanity.

Pope John insisted: the Council must do more than echo the teachings of the past; the world expected much more. To proclaim the Gospel in the modern age, he argued, the faith of the Church "should be studied and expounded through the methods of research and through the literary forms of modern thought."[19] Carefully distinguishing between the perennial "substance" of the faith, and "the way in which it was presented," he maintained that the form of the Church's faith required renewal if the Council was to achieve its pastoral purpose.[20] Like previous ecumenical councils, Vatican II would be concerned to reaffirm Christian doctrine and to address errors. Yet it would not do so by means of legislative texts nor by the declaration of anathemas. For Pope John, the "salient point" of the Council would be to find a way of presenting Church doctrine that corresponded to modern ways of thinking. The Council would teach by means of inspiration, using the language of charity and mercy rather than of condemnation. Similarly, it would call on the whole church to carry out its mission through the persuasive language of authentic witness and service to the human community. The council was to value dialogue far more than confrontation, invitation more than condemnation.

## A Deepened Understanding of the Pastoral Office of the Bishop

Much debate has ensued in recent years regarding the correct interpretation of the Council. While some would argue that Vatican II represents an attenuation of tradition, others insist on the need to understand it as an instance in the legitimate development of doctrine.[21] Beneath this debate lies a failure to appreciate the extent to which the Second Vatican Council represents a significant development and reform in the understanding and exercise of the pastoral teaching office itself. During the conciliar debate, when bishops gave their reasons for rejecting the preparatory texts or asking for substantial revision, they frequently argued that the drafts lacked the pastoral character that John XXIII had called for in his opening speech. They even called for the preparation of a *Pastoral* Constitution on the Church in the Modern World, planting the seeds for what became a text without parallel in conciliar teaching, *Gaudium et Spes*.[22] Yet nowhere did they suggest that in adopting a more pastoral and engaging style of discourse they were abandoning their role as judges of the faith and teachers of Christian doctrine.

The pastoral character of Vatican II's teaching does not imply that the documents have no doctrinal content or that they have lesser value than the teaching of previous ecumenical councils. Arguing that the pastoral and doctrinal dimensions of the Council's teaching were inseparable, Gérard Philips would write, "The pastoral perspective is not something added on to the exposition of doctrine. It is inherent to that exposition, because the truth is essentially destined to be lived, and thus cannot be confined to a theoretical knowledge. This is why a separate treatment of doctrine and practice leads to a sort of vivisection that would be the death of the message's fruitfulness."[23] The sixteen documents of Vatican II contain a number of significant doctrinal developments and take great pains to express the doctrinal self-understanding of the Catholic Church, its ministries, and its mission in the world, in terms that are at once traditional and more accessible to modern people—to both believers and nonbelievers. Indeed, the Pastoral Constitution on the Church in the Modern World, *Gaudium et Spes,* addresses itself to all of humanity—a first in conciliar history.[24]

To renew the Church's teaching and practice, the bishops of Vatican II sought to carry out an important balancing act and to do the work of both *ressourcement,* returning to the sources of the Gospel and of the Christian tradition, and of *aggiornamento*—updating, renewing, and reforming Church teaching and practice so that it might better communicate that faith tradition to contemporaries. The teaching office of the bishops is to maintain the Church in the faith of the apostles, those first witnesses to the Resurrection of Christ. This entails a twofold task. First, they are to preserve the tradition of the Gospel. The second related task is to bring the Gospel to life for contemporary people in every new context. The church is called to mediate a timeless truth in a changing social, cultural, and historical context.

In its reflections on the exercise of authority in the Church, the Anglican-Roman Catholic International Commission refers to the pastoral task of the bishops as a "ministry of memory," suggesting a ministry with an anamnetic character.[25] Its remembering would not be complete were it simply to look back to the historical past. It must also make the tradition actual in the now. That is to say, while the pastoral teaching office has a conservative function—that of ensuring that the life of the community maintains fidelity with the ancient faith and witness of the apostles in the past—it also has a creative role to play as it seeks to actualize that tradition and nourish the living faith of the Church in the present. This creative tension gave birth to a distinctively dialogical style of teaching at Vatican II. Where previous councils may have placed greater emphasis on the conservative function of the bishops' teaching office, the bishops at Vatican II were acutely aware of the need to exercise their creative responsibility in speaking to the modern world.

## Collegial Leadership of the Council: The Coordinating Commission

Pope John did not determine the direction of the Council alone. The story of the Council reveals its remarkably collegial leadership. After the rather poorly coordinated efforts of the Preparatory Theological Commission, which had virtually refused all collaboration with other preparatory commissions and the new Secretariat for Christian Unity, Pope John established a Coordinating Commission to better organize and guide the plan of the Council's deliberations. Already in his historic opening address, John XXIII expressed a view held by a number of visionary bishops who would play important roles in the course of the Council.[26] They shared his serious reservations regarding the approach taken in the draft documents brought forward by the Preparatory Commission.[27] The ten preparatory commissions had submitted more than seventy draft texts, many of them in a tone and style that failed to correspond to John XXIII's directives, however vague they might have been. In May of 1962, Cardinal Suenens of Belgium began to promote a plan to better organize the Council's work. He conferred with Pope John and held a meeting of several cardinals in Belgium in July 1962. Cardinal Frings, of Cologne, suggested the establishment of a subcommission to give a more organic structure to the material to be presented to the Council Fathers. Cardinal Paul-Émile Léger of Montreal addressed a now famous letter to John XXIII in August of 1962, cosigned by the Cardinals Joseph Frings (Cologne), Julius Döpfner (Munich), Franz König (Vienna), Léon-Joseph Suenens (Malines-Brussels), Bernard Alfrink (Utrecht), and Achille Liénart (Lille), all of whom would help determine the Council's direction. Pope John's opening speeches repeat many of the themes from that letter. Léger feared that the Council might turn out to be a dismal failure if it adopted the style reflected in a number of significant schemata.[28] Léger's concerns might be summed up in his comment on the schema on the Magisterium of the Church

(*De Ecclesiae Magisterio*) when he writes, it "proposes a magisterium of security and of conservation rather than a magisterium whose primary responsibility is to announce the Gospel."[29] In short, it showed no regard for the receivers of the Church's proclamation and witness.

Cardinal Suenens's plan, formally placed before the Council Fathers *in aula* on December 4, 1962, also proposed a more positive and pastoral approach to the Council's doctrinal teaching. The hallmark of the plan was the organization of the Council's deliberation along two axes: the first being the inner life and nature of the Church, or the Church *ad intra*—the center of which would be a Dogmatic Constitution on the Mystery of the Church (*Lumen Gentium*); and the second being the "external relations" of the Church, so to speak, the Church *ad extra*, to be contained in an entirely new document, On the Church and the Modern World (*Gaudium et Spes*). Suenens insisted that "the church must engage in a threefold dialogue: (1) with her own believing members; (2) with the 'not yet visibly united brothers' (ecumenism); (3) with the modern world."[30] This plan would largely guide the work of the conciliar commissions for the remainder of the Council.

Giovanni Battista Montini, the Cardinal Archbishop of Milan, supported Suenens's plan. Following his election as Pope Paul VI in June of 1963, he gave expression to a growing consensus among the bishops concerning the priority of the practice of dialogue for the life of the Church, proposing that the language and the practice of dialogue become the Council's leitmotif. His reflections are contained in the first and much neglected encyclical letter of his pontificate, *Ecclesiam Suam*, on the ways in which the Church must carry out its mission.[31]

Pope Paul laid out a threefold program for the Second Vatican Council and for the subsequent activity of the Church. First, he noted the need for a deeper self-understanding of the Church, in particular of its nature and mission. The self-identity of the Church must include a healthy realism about the dissonance between the "ideal image" of the Church intended by Christ, and the "actual image" presented by the community of believers in the world today (*Ecclesiam Suam*, 10). Second, an honest and humble self-examination must lead the Church to undertake whatever reforms deemed necessary for the renewal of its life and witness. The work of *metanoia*, or conversion (*Ecclesiam Suam*, 51), must become a permanent concern as the Church grows in its understanding of the Gospel and in fidelity to its message. The third course of action in Pope Paul VI's overarching vision is dialogue, "friendly dialogue" both within the Church and with the modern world. Pope Paul's vision is clearly one of authority as service exercised through dialogical engagement in a spirit of humility and solidarity with others.

Archbishop Léon-Joseph Suenens (Mechelen-Brussels) and Pope Paul VI. Suenens worked closely with both Pope John XXIII and Pope Paul VI and in 1963 was appointed as one of the four moderators of the Council. Courtesy of Doris Donnelly. (Cardinal Suenens Center at John Carroll University)

John O'Malley has helpfully drawn our attention to the literary genre that distinguishes the sixteen documents of the Second Vatican Council from the style of teaching characteristic of previous ecumenical councils. He argues convincingly that to understand the Council's teaching, we must attend to both what the Council said and to how it said it, or its form of teaching. The Council adopted an epideictic or illustrative form of discourse, in contrast to the controversial or polemical style that had characterized much of Catholic theology and teaching since the Protestant Reformation. This panegyric style recalls the rhetoric of the great Greek and Roman classics, as well as the discourse of many early Christian writings. It paints an idealized portrait in an effort to inspire and incite emulation, to reach the human heart and move it to act.

As O'Malley observes, a new style of discourse required the acquisition of a new vocabulary: the use of "horizontal words" to describe relationships in the Church such as "brother and sister" or "people of God"; "reciprocity words" such as "cooperation," "partnership," and "collaboration."

He notes the frequent use of "friendship words" like the "human family," and of "humility words," such as "pilgrim people." Among the two most important words O'Malley notes the terms "collegiality" and "dialogue." He writes, "'Dialogue' manifests a radical shift from the prophetic I-say-unto-you style that earlier prevailed and indicates something other than unilateral decision-making." He observes further, "there is scarcely a page in the council documents on which 'dialogue' or its equivalent does not occur."[32] In adopting this form of discourse for the teaching of Christian doctrine, the Second Vatican Council effectively committed the Catholic Church to a different style of being church, one in which the exercise of authority and decision making would require learning the habits of charity, mutual respect, and collegiality. It would demand the cultivation of the habits that accompany genuine dialogue, including those of humble self-examination and a readiness to undertake continual reform.

Dialogue in the Church

Perhaps the strongest exhortation to dialogue within the Church can be found in the Council's Pastoral Constitution on the Church in the Modern World. It is worth citing at length because it links the practice of dialogue to the heart of the Church's calling:

> By virtue of her mission to shed on the whole world the radiance of the Gospel message, and to unify under one Spirit all [people] of whatever nation, race or culture, the Church stands forth as a sign of that [fellowship] which allows honest dialogue and gives it vigor. Such a mission requires in the first place that we foster within the Church herself mutual esteem, reverence and harmony, through the full recognition of lawful diversity. Thus all those who compose the one People of God, both pastors and the general faithful, can engage in dialogue with ever abounding fruitfulness. For the bonds which unite the faithful are mightier than anything dividing them. (*Gaudium et Spes*, 92)

This text must be read against the background of *Lumen Gentium*'s insistence that the Church be a sign and a sacrament of the unity and communion that God intends for all of humanity (*Lumen Gentium*, 1). In other words, if the Church wishes to promote dialogue and unity among the nations, its inner life must be a model of that dynamic exchange which nourishes communion.

Behind this commitment to dialogue, which is to characterize the relationships among the faithful within the Church, but also with those outside the visible boundaries of the Catholic Church—including other Christians, other religions, atheists, and all of humanity—lay a new consciousness of the dignity of the human person. John XXIII had pointed to this growing awareness in contemporary society in his opening speech to the Council Fathers. The recognition of the dignity of the human person provided the foundation for the Council's Decree on Religious Freedom, *Dignitatis Humanae*, without which the commitment to dialogue in the Decree on Ecumenism, *Unitatis Redintegratio*, and the Declaration on the Relationship of the Church to Non-Christian Religions, *Nostra Aetate*, would have little credibility. *Dignitatis Humanae* eschews all forms of proselytism and coercion in matters of faith. While maintaining the responsibility of all to pursue the truth, it affirms the right of every person to follow the dictates of his or her conscience. It is in the Decree on Religious Freedom that we find a presentation of dialogue as a common search for the truth (*Dignitatis Humanae*, 3).[33]

## The Exercise of Authority within the Communion of all the Baptized Faithful

The growing awareness of the dignity of each person is undoubtedly at play, however unconsciously, in the Council's recognition of the dignity of all the baptized faithful, and in its elaboration of the rights and responsibilities of the laity (*Lumen Gentium*, 37).[34] These rights are further developed in the 1983 revised Code of Canon Law. In the context of the Church understood as a communion of believers, dialogical engagement is required by respect for the dignity and the value of each member of the ecclesial body. Dialogue is required to nourish the communion that exists among all baptized faithful, to discern and receive the unique contributions and charisms of each.

One of the most noteworthy revisions to the draft text of *Lumen Gentium* that took place in the course of the conciliar debates was the decision to reverse the order of chapters two and three. In the original draft, the chapter on "the hierarchical constitution of the church and the episcopate in particular" preceded a chapter on "the people of God and the laity in particular." Cardinal Suenens and the Coordinating Commission suggested this restructuring of the schema so that an extended reflection on the people of God, or all the baptized faithful, would preface any consideration of the differing vocations and charisms of Christian life: ordained, laity, and religious—all of which were now to be understood under the overarching theme of the universal call to holiness.

In what might be considered a reflection on the dignity of all baptized faithful, chapter 2 of *Lumen Gentium* is almost entirely devoted to an extended consideration of the priestly people of God. By virtue of their baptism, all are said to participate in the priestly, prophetic, and royal offices of Christ. All are called to holiness by offering the sacrifice of their daily living after the example of Christ. Every baptized Christian is called to witness to Christ in word and deed. All are equally called to collaborate in the coming of God's reign.

Reflecting on the prophetic office, article 12 recognizes that the Holy Spirit is given to all baptized faithful and awakens in them an instinct or sense of faith (*sensus fidelium*), a God-given capacity to recognize the truth of the Gospel and to hand it on faithfully to others. It is this gift of the Spirit which grounds the infallible nature of the Church's faith. A renewed understanding of how the *sensus fidelium* includes "the bishops down to the last of the faithful," in the words of Augustine,[35] enables us to understand that the whole people of God is entrusted with the care of God's revelation. This implies that in the exercise of their teaching office, the bishops must attend to the voice of the faithful and to their "supernatural discernment" whenever they are called on to teach on matters of faith. They must be listeners and learners, actively discerning the living faith of the Church, before they can act as authoritative teachers. Their teaching is nothing other than an authoritative witness to the faith of the church in its entirety.

The effect of the Council's decision to place *Lumen Gentium*'s treatment of the priestly people of God before its teaching on the hierarchy serves to situate the exercise of authority by all ordained ministers, in particular the pastoral office of the bishop, within the context of the whole people of God. The ordained are first members of the people of God, and their ministry is to be exercised as a service to the baptized faithful (*Lumen Gentium*, 18). This teaching is summed up in the catechism of the Catholic Church when it observes: "While the common priesthood of the faithful is exercised by the unfolding of baptismal grace—a life of faith, hope, and charity, a life according to the Spirit—the ministerial priesthood is at the service of the common priesthood. It is directed at the unfolding of the baptismal grace of all Christians."[36] Bishops are to act as "brothers" of the laity, and to take as their own the words of Saint Augustine, cited in *Lumen Gentium* (32): "What I am for you terrifies me; what I am with you consoles me. For you I am a bishop; but with you I am a Christian. The former is a duty; the latter a grace. The former is a danger; the latter, salvation."[37]

## Collegiality and the Exercise of Authority by the Episcopate

One of the most contentious debates at the Second Vatican Council was that relating to the collegial nature of *episcope*, or the ministry of oversight exercised by the bishops. The First Vatican Council had been suspended in 1870, immediately following the vote on the definition of papal infallibility, and before the Council Fathers could complete their deliberations on the nature of the episcopal office, which figured high on the agenda. This meant that Vatican I's brief Constitution on the Church (*Pastor Aeternus*) remained a truncated text.[38] An unintended effect of its promulgation was the spread of an overly papal-centered ecclesiology, one that eclipsed the coresponsibility of the episcopate and the diversity of the local churches.

Many assumed, incorrectly, that since Vatican I had so exalted the authority of the pope in affirming his jurisdiction over the local churches, that bishops were reduced to little more than functionaries, or "branch plant managers," whose authority was delegated by the pope for the administration of the life of each diocese. Otto von Bismarck, the German chancellor, published a document in 1872 in which he described the Catholic bishops as mere agents of the pope. In 1875, the German bishops published a rebuttal of Bismarck's contentions with the full support of Pope Pius IX, declaring, "It is a complete misunderstanding of the Vatican decrees to believe that because of them 'episcopal jurisdiction has been absorbed into the papal' . . . [or] 'that the bishops are now no more than tools of the pope.'" Further, they pointed out that the source of the authority belonging to the Bishop of Rome was the same as their own, namely, the episcopal office, and that not even the pope could alter the rights and duties that belonged to their ministry by divine right.[39]

Vatican II sought to redress the imbalance left by Vatican I which had given rise to widespread misunderstandings and to views not unlike those of Bismarck. The teaching of the Second Vatican Council underlines the coresponsibility of all bishops through their ministry of unity within and among the local churches and their solicitude for the universal Church. The Council teaches that "as members of the episcopal college and legitimate successors of the apostles, by Christ's arrangement and decree, each is bound to be solicitous for the entire church" (*Lumen Gentium*, 23).

The Latin term *collegium* is taken from the writings of the early church fathers who spoke of the participation of each bishop in the *corpus episcoporum*.[40] The episcopal college is compared by way of analogy to the group of apostles that surrounded Peter in the New Testament. In light of the biblical witness, which presents Peter as both a member of the apostolic group and a leading figure among them,[41] the Bishop of Rome is understood as both a member and the head of the college. While Vatican II reaffirms the supreme universal power of the Bishop of Rome over the whole church, it implies that he may not act apart from the communion of all the bishops in the "apostolic college." Conversely, the entire college is said to enjoy "supreme and full authority over the universal church," although it has no authority apart from communion with the pope, the college's head (*Lumen Gentium*, 22). There are not two competing authorities, as a number of bishops had feared, but one collegial body acting at times collectively and at other times through its head.[42] As each bishop represents a local church, the college of bishops expresses the communion of churches.

While I have suggested that the experience of the Council itself provides an important example of the collegial exercise of authority in the Church, the interactions between the conciliar assembly and Pope Paul VI, in particular surrounding the debate on collegiality, offer a clue to the somewhat mitigated reception it has received in the intervening years. On October 30, 1963, a historic straw vote was taken on the principle of collegiality. It passed by 1,808 to 336 votes, with 85 percent of the votes in favor. The next day Cardinal Ottaviani, the head of the Holy Office and of the Doctrinal Commission, indicated that he did not accept this as a legitimate vote. A small but determined group of opponents mounted a fierce resistance to the doctrine of collegiality, fearing that it would amount to a concession of authority to the bishops and a diminishment of the papal office. Chapter 3 of *Lumen Gentium* was the subject of more votes than any other council text: forty-one votes in all.[43] The Council presidents provided opportunities to deliberate on the most controversial sections of the text line by line, seeking to obtain as much consensus as possible. Throughout this process, the opposition worked in the wings. O'Malley observes that during the Council's third session, the center of conciliar activity shifted from the hall of Saint Peter's to the papal apartments, as bishops opposed to the direction of the Council beat a path to the pope's door.[44]

Tensions rose to a crescendo in the final week of November 1964, known to many as the "black week" (*settimana nera*). It saw the introduction by a "higher authority" of a qualifying text that had neither been debated nor voted on by the Council relating to the doctrine of collegiality (*Nota Praevia Explicativa*).[45] A series of papal initiatives, undoubtedly aimed at strengthening consensus, had the undesired effect of undermining what might have been a truly collegial exercise of authority.[46] Albert

Outler, an official observer for the Methodists at Vatican II, summed up the consternation of bishops and observers alike:

The closing week of session three was widely regarded as a disaster by all the progressives—Catholics and Protestants alike. It began with the addition, under papal pressure, of a *nota praevia explicativa* to chapter three of the Constitution on the Church which beclouded the clear force of the doctrine of collegiality in the text. This was followed by a papal intervention that qualified the openness toward the Protestants in the draft of the Decree on Ecumenism already approved, penultimately, by the bishops. Further dismay came when the immobilist minority persuaded the presidency to defer a vote on religious liberty—and were upheld in this by the Pope. This series of victories allowed the immobilists by Paul VI was climaxed on the closing day when, in a plainly paraconciliar act, he added the phrase *Mater Ecclesiae* to the "Marian privileges," even though this same controverted phrase had been deliberately omitted from chapter eight of the Constitution on the Church by the (conservative) theological commission itself.[47]

While Outler did not doubt Paul VI's belief in the doctrine of collegiality, he wrote, "one might, however, wonder if he has, as yet, understood or fully accepted what the doctrine implies in practice."[48] The paraconciliar actions of Pope Paul, including his editorializing of texts that had already been voted on by the conciliar assembly, seem to belie a genuine practice of collegiality. It would take time for the theology of collegiality to be received into the life of the Church. The Dominican *peritus* (or theological advisor to the Council) Yves Congar, noting the damage done to ecumenical relationships by these events, writes, "The Pope, who is a man for all, wanted to give satisfaction to all. But in doing this he has come to appear like someone who cannot be fully trusted. Once again, he has neither the theology, nor the intellectual backing for his gestures."[49]

## The Postconciliar Reception of Collegiality

In the end, there were only five negative votes against *Lumen Gentium*. The principle of collegiality entered into official Catholic teaching with almost unanimous support. Its reception would depend largely on the structuring of ecclesial communion that followed the Council in the revision of the Code of Canon Law. In its Decree on the Pastoral Office of the Bishop, *Christus Dominus*, the Council mandated the creation of two new structures intended to embody the collegial exercise of authority in the Church, namely, the synod of bishops (*Christus Dominus*, 5) and the episcopal conferences (*Christus Dominus*, 35, 5; 38, 1–5). The manner in which they came to birth, however, was a portent of how they would be received.

Metropolitan Maximos IV Saigh, the Patriarch of the Melkites and a proponent of collegiality, argued during the Council that the Roman Curia had overextended its proper reach and had usurped a role that belonged to the bishops in the daily governance of the Church. He proposed the creation of a "sacred college of the universal church," a *synodos endimousa*, that is to say, a permanent synod composed of patriarchs and bishops representing the worldwide Catholic communion, who would collaborate with the Bishop of Rome, the Patriarch of the West, and the head of the episcopal college in church governance.[50] He hoped to see this body function as a permanent "executive and judicial council of the universal church." The draft text of *Christus Dominus* contained a provision for the establishment of an international synod of bishops.

But before it could even be discussed, Pope Paul established a synod and determined its parameters by a personal initiative.[51] As it has evolved, the international synod of bishops remains largely an instrument of the papacy. The pope convenes the synod as he sees fit, ratifies its membership, and determines its agenda (*Codex Iuris Canonici*, 344).[52] While the pope retains the prerogative of "endowing it with deliberative power" (*Codex Iuris Canonici*, 343), this has not occurred in the forty-five years of the synod's existence. Today it remains a purely consultative body.

Ironically, since the end of the Second Vatican Council, the College of Cardinals has become a more international body of counselors and assistants to the pope, and functions as a juridical body. It has a special responsibility to elect the Bishop of Rome, but it also assumes an interim governing role on the death of a pope. The Code of Canon Law refers to the cardinalate as a "special college" (*Codex Iuris Canonici*, 349), deliberately avoiding the use of the term "senate." Nonetheless, it has become increasingly common to hear the College of Cardinals spoken of as "the Senate of the Church."[53] The College of Cardinals was never intended as a governing body in the universal church. It was founded in the Middle Ages as an electoral college drawn from the deacons and presbyters of the city of Rome, to take the election of the Bishops of Rome out of the hands of secular princes and nobility.

One may rightly ask whether today, in the absence of an effective synodality within the universal Catholic Church, it has not begun to take on some of these functions. In any case, such a development only seems to confirm the need for an effective collegial body to collaborate with the Bishop of Rome in the exercise of primacy in service to the communion of the local churches. While there may be pragmatic reasons for such an evolution—including the rapid expansion and growing diversity of the worldwide Catholic Church— this development points to an ecclesiological confusion that must soon be addressed.

While bishops in some countries had begun to organize themselves collegially prior to Vatican II, the Council mandated the creation of episcopal conferences in every region. The conferences of bishops were conceived along the lines of the regional synods in the early church (*Christus Dominus*, 36). The Council also encouraged a return to the practice of holding particular councils in each region. To date, only two of these have occurred (in the Philippines and in India). The 1985 Synod of Bishops, which met on the twentieth anniversary of the close of Vatican II, requested a clarification of the theological status of the conferences. Both the collegial nature and the parameters of their functioning were greatly circumscribed by the Apostolic Letter *Apostolos Suos*, issued by Pope John Paul II in 1998.[54] According to this interpretation of the Council's teaching, conferences of bishops make for little more than friendly associations of bishops. One may speak of a binding exercise of authority only when they act unanimously, or when decisions taken by a majority of two-thirds or more are confirmed by the Bishop of Rome. Truly effective collegial acts can only be exercised when the entire college acts in unison—in an ecumenical council, or whenever the pope determines that such an act has occurred in the course of exercising their ordinary universal magisterium. The criteria for arriving at such a determination remain unclear.[55]

Vatican II had sought to redress an imbalance in the understanding of ecclesial authority between papal primacy and episcopal collegiality. While it took significant steps toward doing so, it has clearly not yet achieved a balance that would seem to honor the dignity of each bishop as a vicar of Christ (*Lumen Gentium*, 27), or of the local churches as churches in the full sense of the word. John Wilkins has observed in a recent issue of *Commonweal* magazine, like Bismarck in the nineteenth century, that there are still reasons to ask whether our pastors are truly bishops, or simply "branch managers."[56]

Stephen Schloesser has noted the significance of cultural and geopolitical shifts in shaping the Council's reflections on questions of ecclesial authority: "Postwar decolonization catalyzed this radically new understanding of the Church's relationship to the world. Instead of imposing a unitary ultramontanist culture, 'inculturation' would be seen as a future imperative. . . . Unity replaced uniformity as the guiding principle."[57] In the twenty-first century, tensions between the center and the periphery and the need for an increased commitment to inculturation are felt even more acutely. The unparalleled expansion and increased diversity of the global Catholic population are testing our understanding of unity in catholicity. Pope Francis, the first pope elected from the global South, has noted the need for a "pastoral and missionary conversion" of ecclesial structures to redress an overly centralized mode of church governance and has indicated a clear intention to reform synodal structures and effect a greater devolution of decision making to national and regional conferences of bishops. In contrast to the position of *Apostolos Suos*, he invites a reconsideration of the teaching authority of the episcopal conferences.[58]

## Participation of All Baptized Faithful

Vatican II supported the participation of the laity in diocesan synods and in newly created permanent pastoral councils whenever possible (*Christus Dominus*, 27; *Ad Gentes*, 30; *Codex Iuris Canonici*, 511–14) so that qualified persons might work collaboratively with the bishop to determine the pastoral needs and priorities of the diocese. The ecclesiology that underpins these initiatives extends to the level of the parish, where the parish pastoral council provides a forum for shared reflection and collaboration in parish pastoral planning (*Codex Iuris Canonici*, 536). Yet these structures, too, remain facultative, dependent on the initiative of the bishop or parish pastor. All are intended as instances of consultation, dialogue, and decision making where together we might continue to discern the demands of Gospel living and the shape of the Church's mission in the service of the human family. Implementation has for the most part proven halfhearted or minimalist, to the point that few lay Catholics experience themselves today as taking part in any meaningful conversation regarding matters of consequence for the life of their church. Here as well, Pope Francis recognizes the need for a more robust implementation of participatory structures at every level of ecclesial life.

## Structures of Communion and the Prospects for Ecclesial Unity

I mentioned earlier the reactions of an astute ecumenical observer at Vatican II, a distinguished professor of Duke University, Albert Outler. In his reactions to events at the Council, we can begin to discern the ecumenical implications of the actual exercise of ecclesial authority within the

Catholic Church. The updating and reform of the Catholic Church was to be carried out in view of the "ultimate" (if not immediate) goal of the Council, namely, the restoration of the full, visible unity of the Christian churches.[59] It is no coincidence that through the means of official dialogue among the churches at all levels since the Council we have discovered sometimes surprising levels of consensus on the theology of grace and the sacraments, and uncovered deep divergence in matters of ecclesiology. The vexing question of ecclesial authority—especially the nature of primacy and collegiality, the synodal structuring of the Church, the important role of the *sensus fidelium* in ecclesial decision making—has been the object of protracted study in the context of ecumenical dialogue.[60] While much agreement has been uncovered in the theological understanding of these matters, our differing ecclesial praxis—or perhaps the gaps between our stated theologies and actual practice—remain a serious obstacle to our growing together in communion. Pope Francis suggests that the Catholic Church has much to receive and to learn about synodality from other Christian churches.[61]

The exercise of authority and the question of church order directly relates to the structuring of communion. Whether and how these ecclesial structures enable us to honor the full dignity and charism of each member of the baptized faithful and the concrete uniqueness of each local church within the wider communion is a reflection of how the bonds of communion might be lived out in a reconciled church. Structures for participation and decision making in the Church exist to nourish and protect the communion of charisms shared by all the baptized.

The church and the world of the twenty-first century are vastly different than they were fifty years ago when the Council convened in Rome. The global Catholic population has since doubled, with two-thirds of Catholics now residing in the southern hemisphere. The sheer size and cultural diversity of global Catholicism should serve as an indication of the need for a greater devolution of responsibilities to the regional and local levels. In the discussion that surrounded the recent conclave that elected Pope Francis, we heard frank discussion among Catholic leaders of the need to continue to reform structures of church governance and to correct the balance between the exercise of authority at the center and at the periphery, or between the Bishop of Rome and the bishops in the local churches, in all of their diversity. As we continue to receive the wisdom of the Second Vatican Council, we must go on asking what structures this new millennium will require to enhance the discernment of the Spirit in the Church. The future of the Church, its unity, and its capacity for mission depend on our willingness to create effective spaces for the working of God's Spirit.

1. Second Vatican Council, "Dogmatic Constitution of the Church (*Lumen Gentium*)," 22, in Tanner, *Decrees of the Ecumenical Councils*, 2:866. All citations of the Council documents are taken from Tanner, *Decrees of the Ecumenical Councils*, 2 vols. The college of bishops, understood as acting with and under the Bishop of Rome, who is both member and head of the college, is subject of the supreme authority in the Church. The college of bishops and the pope, both said to exercise supreme authority (*Lumen Gentium*, 23 and 25), are not two distinct subjects, but form one complex subject. Karl Rahner, commenting on the balance of collegial and primatial authority, states: "Juridically speaking, there is only one wielder of supreme power: the college constituted under the Pope as its primatial head. This does not exclude, but rather implies, that the Pope for his part can act 'alone' as primate, since in such an action he need not make use of a regularly constituted collegial act in the strict sense. But even so, he always acts *as* head of the college . . . every primatial action of the Pope contains *de facto* reference to the college as a whole." Rahner, "Dogmatic Constitution on the Church, Chapter III," 1:203.

2. Lafont, *Imagining the Catholic Church*, 2, asks, "Which non-Catholic Church would dare to enter into full communion with the Catholic Church structured as it is at this moment?"

3. *Lumen Gentium*, 18, in Tanner, *Decrees of the Ecumenical Councils*, 2:862–63. The Dominican theologian Yves Congar has written that perhaps the greatest turning point in Western ecclesiology occurred when, in the effort to reform church governance and structures and gain independence from the interference of temporal powers, Pope Gregory VII (1073–85) and his canonists introduced a framework for understanding ministry and the episcopate no longer in sacramental but in juridical terms, as an exercise of power. See his *L'église de Saint Augustin à l'époque moderne*, 103.

4. Second Vatican Council, "Dogmatic Constitution on Divine Revelation, *Dei Verbum*," 10, in Tanner, *Decrees of the Ecumenical Councils*, 2:975.

5. Lafont, *Imagining the Catholic Church*, 37–64.

6. Second Extraordinary Synod (1985), "The Final Report: Synod of Bishops," 444–50.

7. O'Malley, "Vatican II: Did Anything Happen?"

8. Rahner, "Basic Theological Interpretation of the Second Vatican Council," 77–89.

9. Alberigo and Komonchak, *History of Vatican II*, 2:583; cf.1: xii and 4: 327.

10. Lesegretain, "Jean Guitton, premier laïc à parler au concile." Guitton addressed the Council Fathers on December 3, 1963. For a reflection of his thought at the time, see Guitton, *The Church and the Laity*; Guitton, *Dialogues avec Paul VI*.

11. Keegan spoke on October 13, 1964, during the hundredth general congregation of the Council. See Keegan, "Address of Mr. Patrick Keegan." See also "Lay Auditors at the Second Vatican Council."

12. McEnroy, *Guests in Their Own House*.

13. Stransky, "The Observers at Vatican Two: A Unique Experience of Dialogue."

14. Outler, *Methodist Observer at Vatican II*, 12.

15. Moorman, *Vatican Observed*, 28.

16. Philips, "Deux tendances dans la théologie contemporaine."

17. O'Malley, "'The Hermeneutic of Reform,'" 522.

18. Pope John XXIII, *Humanae Salutis*, Convocation of the Second Vatican Council, December 25, 1961, in Abbott, *The Documents of Vatican II*, 703.

19. Pope John XXIII, "Pope John's Opening Speech to the Council [*Gaudet Mater Ecclesia*]," in Abbott, *The Documents of Vatican II*, 715.

20. Ibid., 715.

21. For a good overview of the competing narratives, see O'Malley, "Vatican II: Did Anything Happen?"; Faggioli, "Vatican II: The History and the Narratives," 749–67; Faggioli, *Vatican II: The Battle for Meaning*. For a helpful discussion of how the Council itself speaks of its agenda for reform and renewal, see O'Collins, "Does Vatican II Represent Continuity or Discontinuity?"

22. See the English text from the intervention of Cardinal Joseph Suenens on December 4, 1962, published as "A Plan for the Whole Council," in Stacpoole, *Vatican II by Those Who Were There*, 88–105. See also Suenens, *Souvenirs et espérances*, 55–131; Lamberigts and Declerck, "The Role of Cardinal Léon-Joseph Suenens at Vatican II."

23. Philips, "Deux tendances," 237.

24. *Gaudium et Spes*, 1–2, in Tanner, *Decrees of the Ecumenical Councils*, 2:1069. "The joys and hopes, the griefs and the anxieties of the men of this age, especially those who are poor or in any way afflicted, these too are the joys and hopes, the griefs and anxieties of the followers of Christ. Indeed, nothing genuinely human fails to raise an echo in their hearts. . . . this Second Vatican Council, having probed more profoundly into the mystery of the church, now addresses itself without hesitation, not only to the sons of the church and to all who invoke the name of Christ, but to the whole of humanity." The note to article 2 makes specific reference to the precedent established by Pope John XXIII's encyclical letter *Pacem in Terris*, which was addressed to "all men of goodwill."

25. This expression has been pressed into service by the Anglican-Roman Catholic International Commission (ARCIC) in its most recent agreed statement on the exercise of authority in the Church, *The Gift of Authority*, 42: "In its continuing life, the Church seeks and receives the guidance from the Holy Spirit that keeps its teaching faithful to apostolic Tradition. Within the whole body, the college of bishops is to exercise the ministry of memory to this end. They are to discern and give teaching which may be trusted because it expresses the truth of God surely. In some situations, there will be an urgent need to test new formulations of faith." The commission presents the episcopal ministry of memory as complementing the *sensus fidelium* of all baptized, as the whole church is entrusted with the mystery of God's revelation.

26. Lamberigts and Declerck, "The Role of Cardinal Léon-Joseph Suenens at Vatican II," 74. The authors point out parallels between the text of Cardinal Suenens's plan for the Council and John XXIII's radio address of September 11, 1962. For the text of his speech, see *Acta Apostolicae Sedis* 54 (1962): 678–85. See also Routhier, "Les réactions du cardinal Léger à la préparation de Vatican II"; Suenens, "Aux origines du concile Vatican II." I develop a number of these reflections further in "Learning from the Council: A Church in Dialogue."

27. The recently released diaries of Cardinal Roberto Tucci, the secretary of state to Pope John XXIII (published in *La Civiltà Cattolica*) reveal the pope's general concern about the orientations of the preparatory documents sent to the bishops on the eve of the Council. See Magister, "The Council in the Intimate Thoughts of Pope John XXIII."

28. The full text of the letter can be found in Léger, "Lettre inédite du Cardinal Paul-Émile Léger au Pape Jean XXIII en août 1962."

29. Léger, "Lettre inédite," 109.

30. Lamberigts and Declerck, "The Role of Cardinal Léon-Joseph Suenens at Vatican II," 74.

31. Pope Paul VI, "Ecclesiam Suam, Encyclical of Pope Paul VI on the Church."

32. O'Malley, "Vatican II: Did Anything Happen?," 79.

33. *Dignitatis Humanae*, 3, in Tanner, *Decrees of the Ecumenical Councils*, 2:1003: "Truth, however, is to be sought in a manner befitting the dignity and social nature of the human person, namely by free enquiry assisted by teaching and instruction, and by exchange and [dialogue] in which people explain to each other the truth as they have discovered it or as they see it, so as to assist each other in their search."

34. *Lumen Gentium*, 37, in Tanner, *Decrees of the Ecumenical Councils*, 2:879: "The laity have the right, as do all Christians, to receive in abundance from their spiritual shepherds the spiritual goods of the Church, especially the assistance of the word of God and of the sacraments. They should openly reveal to them their needs and desires with that freedom and confidence which is fitting for children of God and brothers in Christ. They are, by reason of the knowledge, competence or outstanding ability which they may enjoy, permitted and sometimes even obliged to express their opinion on those things which concern the good of the Church. When occasions arise, let this be done through the organs erected by the Church for this purpose. Let it always be done in truth, in courage and in prudence, with reverence and charity toward those who by reason of their sacred office represent the person of Christ."

35. Augustine, *On the Predestination of the Saints*, 14, 27, quoted in *Lumen Gentium*, 12, in Tanner *Decrees of the Ecumenical Councils*, 2:858.

36. *Catechism of the Catholic Church*, no. 1547.

37. See Augustine, Sermon 340, 1 quoted in *Lumen Gentium*, 32, in Tanner, *Decrees of the Ecumenical Councils*, 2:876.

38. First Vatican Council, *Pastor Aeternus*, in Tanner, *Decrees of the Ecumenical Councils*, 2:811–16.

39. "Collective Declaration of the German Hierarchy"; Pius IX, "Apostolic Brief of March 6, 1875." Cf. Denzinger and Schönmetzer, *Enchiridion Symbolorum*, 3117.

40. A number of studies produced during the conciliar period trace the history of the term. See, for example, Botte, "La collégialité dans le Nouveau Testament et chez les Pères apostoliques"; Stanley, "The New Testament Basis for the Concept of Collegiality"; Le Guillou, "Le parallélisme entre le Collège apostolique et le Collège épiscopal"; Colson, *L'épiscopat catholique*.

41. See the important study by leading Lutheran and Catholic exegetes: Brown, Donfreid, and Reumann, *Peter in the New Testament*.

42. "It was not a matter of contrasting two rival powers, but of describing the organic union, unique in its kind, which links the supreme head of the church hierarchy with the bishops as a group." Philips, "History of the Constitution," 113.

43. Noted by Ratzinger, *Theological Highlights of Vatican II*, 162.

44. O'Malley, *What Happened at Vatican II*, 205.

45. For an understanding of the origins of this text—a commentary on the amendments, not on the final text of *Lumen Gentium*—drafted for use within the Doctrinal Commission, see Grootaers, *Primauté et collegialité*.

46. A source of some tension throughout the Council, the Council regulations had not made clear how the popes were to relate to the Council. This caused some confusion within the Doctrinal Commission and the Secretariat for Promoting Christian Unity, who found themselves at times constrained by papal "suggestions," while at others did not consider themselves bound by them.

47. Outler, *Methodist Observer at Vatican II*, 76.

48. Ibid., 84.

49. Congar, *My Journal of the Council*, 697.

50. Maximos IV, "The Supreme Senate of the Catholic Church."

51. Pope Paul VI, *Motu proprio Apostolica Sollicitudo*, 794–804. The original draft text from the decree described the role of this "Central Coetus or Council" as follows: "Since the universal mission of the Supreme Pontiff demands greater resources of help and assistance each day, the Fathers of this Holy Council vehemently wish that some bishops from different regions of the world may offer to the supreme Pastor of the Church more effective aid, in a manner to be determined at the proper time, even, if it should please the Supreme Pontiff, coming together in a certain *coetus* or council, which could at the same time be a sign of the participation of all the bishops in solicitude for the universal church." Cf. *Acta Synodalia Sacrosancti Concilii Vaticani II*, III.2: 23–24.

52. Canon Law Society of America, *Code of Canon Law*. All citations are taken from this edition.

53. See, for example, Benedict XVI, "Homily, Ordinary Public Consistory for the Creation of New Cardinals, 25 November 2007."

54. John Paul II, "*Apostolos Suos*."

55. Rahner, commenting on *Lumen Gentium*, 22, in the wake of the Council wrote, "The exercise of the authority of the college must: a) be a collegiate act. That is, it must take place in a legally determined way, to be decided eventually according to the positive human law of the church, so that the decision may appear as the act of the college itself. Then, b) it follows from the nature of the college that the cooperation of the pope is necessary." In Rahner, "Dogmatic Constitution of the Church," 1:200.

56. Wilkins, "Bishops or Branch Managers?"

57. Schloesser, "Against Forgetting," 105.

58. Pope Francis, "Apostolic Exhortation on the Joy of the Gospel (*Evangelii Gaudium*)," especially nos. 25–33.

59. Bea, "The Catholic Attitude towards the Problem [of the Union of Christians]," 36.

60. By way of example, the topic of authority has figured high on the agenda of the Anglican-Roman Catholic International Commission (ARCIC), "Authority in the

Church I and II"; ARCIC, *The Gift of Authority: Authority in the Church III*. See also Groupe des Dombes, *One Teacher*.

61. Pope Francis, "Apostolic Exhortation on the Joy of the Gospel (*Evangelii Gaudium*)," no. 246: "We can learn so much from one another! It is not just about being better informed about others, but rather about reaping what the Spirit has sown in them, which is also meant to be a gift for us. To give but one example, in the dialogue with our Orthodox brothers and sisters, we Catholics have the opportunity to learn more about the meaning of episcopal collegiality and their experience of synodality. Through an exchange of gifts, the Spirit can lead us ever more fully into truth and goodness."

4

# VATICAN II AND THE HISTORY
# OF INTERPRETATION

The Case of Roman Catholic Womenpriests

*Jill Peterfeso*

Although the Roman Catholic Church bars even the discussion of women's ordination, the group known as Roman Catholic Womenpriests (RCWP) started ordaining women in 2002. As of May 2008, all of RCWP's ordained women are excommunicated, but the ordinations persist, with approximately 150 women (and a few men) having been ordained throughout western Europe, North America, parts of South America, and South Africa. In spite of Vatican claims that RCWP's celebrated masses are only "a simulation of a sacrament,"[1] the ordained women work to shepherd Catholic communities, offer Eucharist, and participate in myriad ministerial forms. The Church may insist on mandatory clerical celibacy, but RCWP's ordained women include wives, mothers, and grandmothers, as well as lesbians in committed relationships. RCWP continues to grow, all the while justifying its existence with appeals to Vatican II.[2]

Women's ordination was not on the table at the Second Vatican Council. In fact, one can safely presume that few Catholics prior to Vatican II even envisioned the possibility of female priests.[3] Canon Law 1024 was and remains clear on this point: "Only a baptized male validly receives sacred ordination."[4] The priest's authority is indelibly linked to the Church's well-accepted patriarchal authority, and before Vatican II, few women spoke publicly about aspiring to share in that sacramental power. There was one noteworthy exception: the German theologians Iris Müller and Ida Raming submitted the women's ordination issue to the Council for consideration; their petition was published in a 1964 book compiled by Gertrud Heinzelmann titled, significantly, *We Shall Keep Quiet No More! Women Speak to the Second Vatican Council.*[5] The Council did not take up the issue, however, and conciliar documents reveal no engagement with the question of female priests.

Nor does evidence suggest that Vatican II aimed to reconfigure Catholic women's authority within the Church. Vatican II was by no means a welcoming place for women or women's voices. Only twenty-three women took part in proceedings that involved approximately 2,600 (male) bishops.[6] Women could not attend until the third Council session, and when they did arrive as auditors, they could neither address Council Fathers nor speak publicly.[7] Catherine Clifford's essay in the present volume draws attention to the way Council Fathers consulted with and listened to the concerns of the laity, thereby approaching the idea of a truly "universal" church.[8] Yet Catholic laypersons who had been waiting intently for a greater voice did not see the Council's invitation going far enough. No one felt this lack more strongly than women. The one American woman who attended Vatican II—the Loretto sister Mary Luke Tobin—has said that women there were either "ignored or trivialized."[9] Women were present at Vatican II, but in numbers and impact far smaller than they desired.

And yet, although women's voices and the question of women's ordination were not on the minds of the Council Fathers, clusters of Catholic women began calling for ordination after the Council. To this day, a group like RCWP can be anathema to church teaching while simultaneously pointing to church teaching to validate its existence. RCWP heralds certain Vatican II documents and the conciliar "spirit" to explain its *contra legem* ("against Canon Law") actions. While Vatican II was not the sole force giving rise to either Catholic feminism or formal calls for female priests, I wish to underscore the ways Vatican II fueled an already smoldering situation of 1960s social ferment.[10] When the Vatican II windows cracked open and the winds of *aggiornamento* (updating) began blowing, some women readily seized on what they viewed as newfound opportunities. Secular feminism and civil rights movements combined with Vatican II themes to theologize social change. The Council's silence on the specific issue of womenpriests did not prevent groups of Catholic women from raising the question.

Roman Catholic Womenpriests is heir to early agitations arising from the proto-Catholic feminist stirrings in and around Vatican II. Even though the Roman Catholic hierarchy views RCWP's women as schismatic heretics who reject church teaching, I contend that precisely RCWP's marginal status makes it an invaluable addition to any discussion of the Second Vatican Council's "long shadow." After all, the group deliberately calls itself *Roman* Catholic and connects itself to Vatican II. The present essay uses RCWP as a case study for rethinking contemporary Catholicism, identity politics inherent in hermeneutical approaches to

Vatican II, and the locus of interpretive authority. I ask: Why does a history of Vatican II interpretation and meaning-making matter for those of us who study contemporary Catholicism—particularly marginal American Catholic groups that seem disconnected from formal Church teaching?

This article shows that womenpriests see themselves as living and embodying a feminist, liberative hermeneutical approach to Vatican II. This, in their view, is the only correct way to interpret the Second Vatican Council. Given that RCWP's conclusions about Vatican II have led the group to take extreme action, I argue that historians of Catholicism must continue to reinvestigate their analytical categories and their presuppositions around the Second Vatican Council. As this essay will demonstrate, investigating RCWP's relationship with Vatican II reveals a perhaps unexpected proximity between twenty-first-century Catholic excommunicants and their church's teachings. Certainly, it upends assumptions about the relationship between progressive Catholics and hierarchical authority. Focusing on women's ordination activists broadly and on RCWP specifically demonstrates how interpretive history informs religious identity and action among all the faithful—those at the center and those on the margins.

Scholarly Responses to Vatican II

Just because women's ordination activists have interpreted Vatican II in feminist ways does not mean that all Catholics or even most scholars agree on the Council's meaning. There was little consensus in the Council's wake, and there is little consensus now. Underscoring these continued quests for meaning is the fact of extensive and ongoing research about Vatican II. In the past five years, many Council-focused monographs have appeared on the scene—several of them excellent studies by distinguished scholars.[11] In addition, nearly every study that focuses on or arrives at late-twentieth-century or present-day Catholicism broaches the subject of Vatican II, in however cursory or critical a fashion. Not every study needs to become a retrospective on Vatican II, of course, yet authors must continue exercising care in commenting on the Second Vatican Council. Interpretations of conciliar changes remain in the making, with new studies participating in the recasting of Vatican II's historical significance.

Scholars and Vatican observers also continue trying to understand papal views on Vatican II—a deceptively simple task. Most progressive Catholics maintain that Popes Benedict XVI and John Paul II (and some would even add Paul VI) sought to overturn the good work started under John XXIII. This is a familiar refrain in so-called liberal Catholic circles; indeed, an article in the progressive-minded *National Catholic Reporter*'s Vatican II fiftieth-anniversary edition sought to explain how and why Joseph Ratzinger changed positions on Vatican II reforms in the 1960s, transforming from a conciliar supporter to a vociferous challenger.[12] Others contend, however, that Ratzinger never held a clear-cut position. In a 2005 speech to the Roman Curia, Benedict XVI described two ways of interpreting the Second Vatican Council: the "hermeneutics of discontinuity" and the "hermeneutics of reform." Commentators rushed to interpret Benedict's (own interpretive) remarks: those on the right applauded what they understood as the pope expressing discontent with Vatican II changes; those on the left decried what they understood as the pontiff distancing himself from conciliar reforms. At least one scholar, however, argues that neither side understood Benedict's comments correctly: Father Joseph Komonchak contends that the pope was actually emphasizing—and not undermining—reform (i.e., the "hermeneutics of reform") and reasons why change (i.e., "discontinuity") was necessary when John XXIII summoned the Council. Komonchak concludes by noting, if not praising, Benedict's nuanced approach, and calls on scholars to tread more carefully when assessing Council interpretations.[13]

Much is at stake. American Catholicism today appears beset by dualistic divides: liberal versus conservative, progressive versus traditional, left versus right.[14] These are loaded and overly simple terms, and they often obfuscate the issues at the heart of disagreement. The parties involved in the women's ordination debate prove no exception. Each side lays claim to particular interpretations of Vatican II. As Komonchak noted, "history and hermeneutics go together," and thus those who make historical claims automatically make meaning.[15] Polarities in American Catholicism make for convenient binaries, but tidy conclusions belie the complex stories underlying histories of interpretation.

Leslie Tentler's latest research nuances interpretive questions and invites historians to reconceptualize historiographies of Vatican II hermeneutics. When examining racial tensions in 1960s Detroit, Tentler finds that Catholics on *both* sides of the racial debate invoked Vatican II to justify their positions. Individuals who opposed Archbishop John Dearden's attempts to deescalate racial tensions argued that the prelate was being a heavy-handed clergyman, overstepping his authority. These opponents claimed their own rights as newly empowered laypeople—as the "people of God" laid out in *Lumen Gentium*—to stand up to clerical decisions with which they disagreed. On the other side of the debate,

Catholics who supported Dearden's efforts to racially integrate parishes and neighborhoods also used Vatican II to bolster their claims: they applauded Dearden's "openness to the world" and attention to the poor—both themes of Vatican II documents. The year was 1968; Vatican II's liturgical reforms had not yet been fully implemented. And yet it was not long before American Catholics in the Detroit Archdiocese imbibed and implemented Vatican II rhetoric—selectively.[16]

Interpretations of Vatican II have thus been woven into Council fabric from the outset. Debates about what the Council meant and means do not, then, constitute a later development owing to radical feminism, changing sexual mores, or a deepening divide between the Catholic left and the Catholic right. Significantly, Tentler's Dearden example shows that even non-progressive Catholics in Michigan (i.e., those who opposed racial reforms) managed to find support for their views in conciliar documents. Contemporary groups like RCWP may seem to reinforce today's popular view that Vatican II offers ammunition for progressive Catholics only, but as Tentler helps us see, this was not always the case.

Historians must therefore keep pushing at and pulling on the presupposed boundaries around Vatican II and its meaning. When viewed as the organic, evolving processes that they are, the interpretations of Vatican II take on a history of their own, and histories of postconciliar Catholicism can become enriched with hermeneutic diversity spanning the past fifty years. Taking a page from biblical studies proves instructive here: Dale B. Martin has worked to underscore the *"activities of interpretation* by which people 'make meaning' of biblical texts."[17] Any interpretive questions touch on matters of authorial intent and supposed textual truths. Drawing on poststructuralist theories that deny texts any inherent meaning outside of human interpretation, Martin illumines the "agency of human interpreters" over and against the "myth of textual agency."[18] The same could and should be argued for Vatican II documents. Regardless of the conciliar fathers' intent, Vatican II documents have had the impact of offering some groups—women's ordination activists included—the rhetorical tools to move forward with goals that run counter to other church teachings.

This agency of human interpreters has gone further still. Interpretation has not remained limited to textual authority but has been necessarily (and elaborately) connected to ecclesiastical authority. As we will see, by the 1970s, women's ordination activists were prepared to accept and elevate certain Vatican II texts and themes. At the same time, they felt comfortable separating those texts from the Vatican prelates and procedures that had given rise to them. Considering that the women's goal was ordination—something the all-male hierarchy stridently denied—it became necessary to discover legitimate themes within the texts while delegitimizing the ordained men who authored them.

Roman Catholic Womenpriests' own feminist liberative hermeneutic applied to Vatican II takes on a different tone and tenor when we note that, first, Vatican II interpretive moves happened speedily after the Council, and second, conservative (and not just liberal) positions were argued for and upheld using Vatican II documents. RCWP's lineage, when traced back to Vatican II, looks like part of a hermeneutical process—a process in which Catholics of all stripes (left and right, progressive and traditional) could and did take part. RCWP not only roots itself in certain Vatican-expressed sentiments, but the organization's seeds were planted in fertile soil at a time when *many* American Catholics sought to make sense and meaning of Vatican II.

### *Gaudium et Spes:* Joy in Empowerment, Hope for Ordination

Select Vatican II documents fueled activists' fire in the decades following the Council. Like the Detroit-area Catholics Tentler describes, women's ordination activists invoked *Lumen Gentium*'s emphasis on the laity's important role as the "people of God." They also celebrated and cited *Pacem in Terris*'s reflections on conscience; although the latter was a 1963 encyclical written by John XXIII and not one of the sixteen con-ciliar documents, *Pacem in Terris* usually gets swept up in discussions of the spirit of Vatican II and further elevates John XXIII's status in the minds of progressive Catholics.[19] Finally, the document that rises above all others is *Gaudium et Spes*, or "The Pastoral Constitution on the Church in the Modern World," which also elevated conscience and condemned sexism.

As mentioned above, female auditors had little say in Council delibera-tions, but they could participate in developing what would become known as *Gaudium et Spes*. This apostolic constitution sought to bring the Church into harmonious relation with modern life, instructing the Catho-lic faithful on how to discern God's will for humankind.[20] Most important for Catholic feminists, *Gaudium et Spes* condemned all types of discrim-ination, including sexism: "With respect to the fundamental rights of the person, every type of discrimination, whether social or cultural, whether based on sex, race, color, social condition, language, or religion, is to be overcome and eradicated as contrary to God's intent."[21] The document acknowledged the roles that men *and* women play as "the authors and the artisans of the culture of their community."[22] Moreover, women found in *Gaudium et Spes* the inspiration to pursue theological studies, a discipline for which Catholic leaders had historically viewed women as ill-suited. Prior to 1960, Catholic seminaries and universities prohibited women from studying theology; female students were often directed to philosophy instead, seen as similar but less demanding.[23] This shift, compounded with *Gaudium et Spes*, led some to view Vatican pronouncements as an endorsement of female theologians.[24] Women therefore interpreted the document as a correction to years of exclusion.

As Mary J. Henold contends in her 2008 monograph, *Catholic and Feminist*, the honor of being "the immediate catalyst for the emerging [Catholic feminist] movement . . . belongs to the institutional Catholic Church, which itself must take the credit for both provoking and inspiring Catholic feminism in the early sixties throughout the Second Vatican Council."[25] Some Catholic feminists moved speedily toward applying Vatican declarations to their own lives and desires as women in the Church. Advocates for women's ordination seized on Vatican II reforms broadly and *Gaudium et Spes* specifically. The Women's Ordination Conference (WOC) recalls its early history this way: in 1975, "armed with the Second Vatican Council document *Gaudium et Spes*, U.S. Catholic proponents of women's ordination, both women and men . . . began planning what they thought would be a small national meeting for like-minded people, a Women's Ordination Conference, in Detroit, Michigan."[26] Records of the proceedings reveal the frequency with which conference speakers referenced Vatican II, specifically *Gaudium et Spes*, as well as *Pacem in Terris* and the idea of the Church as the people of God.[27] This "small national meeting" drew about two thousand participants, far more than planners had envisioned, and soon developed into an organization. Today, WOC proudly calls itself the "oldest and largest organization" working for women's ordination into an "inclusive and accountable" Roman Catholic Church. The group's website includes a list of the "Top Ten Reasons to Ordain Women," and item nine cites *Gaudium et Spes*: "Every type of discrimination . . . based on sex . . . is to be overcome and eradicated as contrary to God's intent."[28] This group has attracted members worldwide and heralds Vatican II and *Gaudium et Spes* as both inspiration and justification for its provocative actions.

The Women's Ordination Conference is not alone. The London-based group that maintains www.womenpriests.org (Women Can Be

Priests)—"the leading international Catholic online authority on women's ministries"—cites *Gaudium et Spes* on its homepage: "All the faithful, both clerical and lay, should be accorded a lawful freedom of inquiry, freedom of thought and freedom of expression."[29] Freedom of inquiry and expression is essential for this group's mission, because unlike RCWP, Women Can Be Priests do not support the *illegal* ordination of women, and thus want women's ordination to arise from theological and pastoral discussion between the hierarchy and the faithful. This stance signals deference amid resistance: deference to Church teachings alongside resistance to the theological positions barring women's ordination. Similarly, in 2012, the progressive Catholic group Call to Action held a year-long "celebration" of Vatican II, complete with a lecture series, colloquia, and prayer services. On the website announcing the commemorative events, the group cited Pope John XXIII: "It is not that the Gospel has changed, it is that we have begun to understand it better . . . the moment has come to discern the signs of the times, to seize the opportunity to look far ahead."[30] For these progressive Catholic organizations, Vatican II and *Gaudium et Spes* offered in the 1960s and continue offering today road maps to a liberal and liberative Catholic future.

While the bishops participating in Vatican II did not seek to unleash calls for female priests, Council observers made interpretive moves that inspired them to raise questions about female ordination—and ask these questions with increasing volume and velocity. Activist women like those who have pushed for discussion of women's ordination have viewed Vatican II through a feminist, liberative lens, in no small part because of certain phrases and concepts within *Gaudium et Spes*, *Pacem in Terris*, and *Lumen Gentium*. Perhaps tellingly, Vatican II did not offer many documents combating sexism. But *Gaudium et Spes*, in particular, remains distinctive: out of Vatican II's sixteen documents, which tackle a range of topics, women's ordination activists have seized on language decrying sexism in *Gaudium et Spes*. Rhetorically, theoretically, and theologically, this is the document that has served the cause of ordaining women.

## The RCWP Example

The years between Vatican II (1962–65) and RCWP's first ordination (2002) left women's ordination activists with little hope that a change in Canon Law 1024 was forthcoming. With the lone exception of the Pontifical Biblical Commission—which in 1976 concluded that scripture alone did not suffice as evidence for barring women clergy[31]—Vatican

Ordination of three women deacons on May 1, 2010, at Spiritus Christi Church in Rochester, New York. Two women were also ordained priests at this ceremony. In addition to the presiding bishop, Andrea Johnson, selected community representatives laid hands on each ordinand, thus signaling that the call to ministry came from both the bishop and the church as the people of God. (Photo by Jill Peterfeso)

statements opposing women's ordination first appeared and later intensified as advocacy groups like WOC publicly called for female priests. In 1976 (and released in English in January 1977, with the full title of Declaration on the Admission of Women to the Ministerial Priesthood), *Inter Insigniores* stated, "the Church, in fidelity to the example of the Lord, does not consider herself authorized to admit women to priestly ordination." The primary reasons *Inter Insigniores* labeled women priests an impossibility were twofold: Jesus Christ called only men as apostles, and Catholic sacramental economy required the priest to stand *in persona Christi*—specifically, the priest must be able to emulate the *maleness* of Christ.[32] These arguments saddened but did not silence ordination advocates, who suggested *Inter Insigniores*'s newfound theological defense of an all-male priesthood revealed that WOC was, in fact, pushing the right buttons. In 1994, Pope John Paul II issued the Apostolic Letter *Ordinatio Sacerdotalis*, which reiterated *Inter Insigniores*. Toward the letter's end, John Paul II wrote, "I declare that the Church has no authority whatsoever to confer priestly ordination on women and that this judgment is to be *definitively held* by all the Church's faithful" (emphasis added). With this communication, the pope sought to end discussion of women's ordination altogether.[33]

As Vatican pronouncements seemed to further remove ordination activists from their goals, some looked to more dramatic action. By the turn of the twenty-first century, a Catholic woman in Austria named Christine Mayr-Lumetzberger had started a preparation group for women interested in ordination—independent of Church approval. Ida Raming and Iris Müller—the German theologians who had petitioned the Council Fathers to consider women's ordination nearly forty years earlier—connected with Mayr-Lumetzberger. While Raming and Müller had long advocated women's ordination from "within the system" (i.e., through theological discourse and ecclesial discussion), they had grown discouraged and no longer trusted that such transformation would happen within the hierarchy. They came to believe that if Roman Catholic women were going to be ordained, they would have to first do so *contra legem*.[34] So Mayr-Lumetzberger, Raming, Müller, and a number of other women moved forward with their preparations for priesthood. Their greatest challenge lay in finding a bishop to ordain them. Indeed, if they were to claim theirs a "valid but illicit" ordination (i.e., valid in their apostolic succession, illicit in their breaking of Canon Law 1024), they needed episcopal legitimacy. Ultimately, they found three men willing to lay hands on them. While the women's critics scrutinized the ordaining bishops and their qualifications, the women themselves were satisfied that their ordinations met the criteria for validity. On June 29, 2002, on a rented pleasure boat sailing the Danube River, seven women were ordained. They would become known as the "Danube Seven," and their actions would mark the beginning of the movement today known as Roman Catholic Womenpriests.[35]

The movement grew slowly but steadily in the early years. Women were ordained deacons, priests, and then bishops, as some of the male Catholic bishops secretly supporting RCWP encouraged the group to have their own female bishops. This way, the nascent group would no longer need to rely on male prelates—who were risking their careers by supporting the womenpriests—for apostolic succession. The first ordination in North America took place on the St. Lawrence Seaway in 2005. The first ordination in the United States occurred the following year, in Pittsburgh. In the intervening years, RCWP has grown exponentially, with the vast majority of new members coming from the United States.

In the early years, the Vatican responded to the budding movement with threats and warnings. Weeks before the initial ceremony on the Danube, Church officials threatened everyone participating with excommunication—not just the ordinands and officients, but any supporters and journalists in attendance. After the ceremony, however, only the Danube Seven received the Summons and Canonical Admonition, requesting that they repent of their actions. The seven women refused, and the decree of excommunication followed. For several years thereafter, Roman Catholic authorities warned the womenpriests but did not follow through with excommunication. This changed in March 2008, when Elsie McGrath and Rose Marie Hudson received a decree of excommunication from the archbishop of St. Louis, Raymond Burke. They were the first womenpriests to be excommunicated since the Danube Seven.[36] Then in May 2008, the Congregation for the Doctrine of the Faith (CDF) issued a general decree excommunicating all womenpriests *latae sententiae*, meaning the women become automatically severed from the sacraments on attempting ordination, so that a Church leader need not issue a specific, formal decree for each woman.[37] RCWP's women reject excommunication, saying they are "loyal members of the church who stand in the prophetic tradition of holy obedience to the Spirit's call to change an unjust law that discriminates against women."[38] In the years since the 2008 decree, RCWP has gone on to ordain scores of women. The Vatican, for its part, seems to now ignore the movement altogether, letting the 2008 decree speak for the Church.

While RCWP's ordained women seem to stand in strict opposition to the Vatican hierarchy, their actions arise from an affiliation with Vatican teaching: specifically, that of *Gaudium et Spes* and Vatican II. The movement's 2007 Vision Statement announced, "We are called to renew Theology, Liturgy, and Pastoral Practice to better reflect the spirit and teachings of the Second Vatican Council as expressed in *Gaudium et Spes*."[39] The ordained female bishop Bridget Mary Meehan uses a different portion of *Gaudium et Spes* to argue for women's ordination in a 2011 blog post:

Liturgy at the Church of the Beatitudes, Santa Barbara, California. (Photo by Rev. Juanita Cordero)

The *Pastoral Constitution of the Church in the Modern World* 1965 (*Gaudium et Spes*) states clearly that women and men are equals: "All women and men are endowed with a rational soul and are created in God's image; they have the same nature and origin, and, being redeemed by Christ, they enjoy the same divine calling and destiny; there is here a basic equality between all, and it must be accorded ever greater recognition." Sadly, the Vatican and hierarchy in 2011 ignore their own authoritative teaching. The call for the full equality of women in church and society is the voice of God in our times and one that the Second Vatican Council affirmed.[40]

In Meehan's understanding, RCWP and others who support women's ordination are working for gender equality, in keeping with Vatican II directives. The Church and its prelates are the ones failing to grasp the Second Vatican Council's message.

RCWP has also used Vatican II themes to argue against members' excommunications. An RCWP 2009 press release calling on the Vatican to lift the *latae sententiae* excommunication of RCWP's women argues that, in fact, the group affirms and obeys Church teaching: "We stand

Call to Action, November 2011. RCWP-USA Booth in exhibit hall in Milwaukee, Wisconsin. (Photo by Rev. Juanita Cordero)

firmly in the tradition of Vatican II," the release declares, before citing *Gaudium et Spes*'s quotation denouncing sexism.[41] Likewise, in contesting excommunication, RCWP's statements indict the Church for not standing by its own teachings on conscience. When responding to the 2008 excommunication decree, RCWP issued a statement comparing its own acts of conscience to those of Hildegard of Bingen and Joan of Arc, "heroic women in the church's tradition" who put obedience to God above hierarchical subjugation. The group also cites (in order to critique) Pope Benedict XVI, who in the 1960s as Joseph Ratzinger wrote commentary on Vatican II, in which he stated, "Over the Pope as the expression of the binding claim of ecclesiastical authority, there still stands one's own conscience, which must be obeyed before all else, if necessary even against the requirement of ecclesiastical authority."[42] The womenpriests understand theirs as a vocational call, and if obeying God and conscience means disobeying Canon Law, so be it.

If RCWP is going to validate its *contra legem* actions, win public support, and vilify the current Church leadership, the movement has to look back in time, past the 2008 General Decree, past Vatican and local diocesan statements warning the women planning for ordination, and past *Ordinatio Sacerdotalis* and *Inter Insigniores*; RCWP has to find Vatican

support for its actions by claiming a progressive, antisexist, and even egalitarian idea of the Church. The group's members find this where their
foremothers in the women's ordination movement found it: in select
statements and interpretations from Vatican II documents.[43]

As should now be clear, RCWP (and other groups that share a focus on
women's authority in the Church) views Vatican II through a feminist, liberative lens that upholds even RCWP's *contra legem* actions. Müller and
Raming's 2010 autobiographical account of their decades-long struggle
for ordination focuses heavily on Vatican II and is tellingly called *"Contra Legem": A Matter of Conscience.* The womenpriests consider such
radical disobedience acceptable *because* it honors the spirit and intent of
Vatican II, *as* these progressive Catholic movements interpret and understand Vatican II. The gestures of RCWP to 1960s Vatican statements
speak volumes: the ones who misinterpret and misunderstand the "real"
meaning of Vatican II are the individuals from popes down to priests
who fail to implement sweeping reforms. Even now, fifty years after the
Council, RCWP and its ilk will herald Vatican II as the defining moment
for present-day Catholicism. Although the womenpriests have suffered
excommunication, RCWP's rhetorical strategy suggests the opposite: we
women are not the ones who have gone astray; instead, it is the ordained
men in charge who willfully defy the spirit of the Second Vatican Council.

Conclusion

Making interpretive claims about Vatican II was and continues to be part
of American Catholic practice. Scholars, priests, prelates, and laypeople
participate in these efforts—and have since the 1960s. The modes of selective interpretation differ, as do the documents emphasized, but the RCWP
example reveals how Vatican II interpretations continue unfolding, even
fifty years hence. RCWP's own argument from interpretation keeps bringing "joy and hope" (to reference *Gaudium et Spes*) to the excommunicated
womenpriests: when accused of being a new "protestant sect," they argue
that they belong—not just to Christianity writ large but to Rome and
Roman Catholic teachings. They claim to be obedient: RCWP's ordained
align themselves with the institutional Church by vowing, pledging, and
publicly performing adherence to specific Vatican II documents that support conscience and condemn sexism.

These interpretive issues raise valuable questions for scholars, ministers, and practitioners alike. At heart are issues of authority: individual
interpretive authority versus hierarchical, institutional authority. As the

Church opened to the modern world, the Catholic faithful opened as well: to seeing the Second Vatican Council as a potential corrective to all that ailed them. Empowered by a myriad of changes throughout the 1960s—in society and culture, in gender roles and sexual identities, in political systems and Church institutions—many American Catholics seized interpretive authority. Time will tell—and we would do well to watch—how long RCWP (and WOC and other progressive Catholic reform groups) harken back to these Vatican II texts. At some point, will Vatican II become moot for them? Will new statements from Pope Francis replace or reframe John XXIII's? Or will decades of closed doors ultimately see these groups leaving Rome and "Roman" behind altogether?

These questions about hermeneutics and interpretations toward reform remain significant. It is not simply that Vatican II yielded different interpretations, but that Vatican II signals a moment in Catholic history when some Catholics—and specifically here, American Catholic feminists—took ownership of interpretive meaning-making. Previously throughout Catholic history, the Church positioned itself between the faithful and scripture, so as to ensure correct textual understanding. Tentler quips in her essay that, growing up in the 1950s and 1960s, her non-Catholic neighbors "knew for a fact that we [Catholics] could not think for ourselves."[44] With Vatican II, however, some Catholics did begin thinking for themselves. Or, more to the point of this essay, Catholics began to *interpret* for themselves, to uncover their agency as human interpreters. The texts received life through a range of interpretations, leaving today's Church still debating—and today's marginal Catholic groups still experimenting with—the meaning and intent of Vatican II.

NOTES

1. Congregation for the Doctrine of the Faith, "Warning Regarding the Attempted Priestly Ordination of Some Catholic Women."

2. I use the term "Roman Catholic Womenpriests" to refer to the international movement that began with the ordination of the Danube Seven on June 29, 2002. The group did not use this name until it came to North America in 2005. In German-speaking Europe today, the group is known as "Römish-katholische Priesterinnen" and "Initiative Weiheämter für Frauen in der römish-katholischen Kirche." RCWP is related to the Association of Roman Catholic Womenpriests (ARCWP), which formed out of RCWP in 2010. The movement is unified yet made up of regional groups with some differences in governance and ministerial approaches. "RCWP," then, is an umbrella term at best.

3. We do know that nineteenth-century Saint Thérèse of Lisieux longed to be a priest. While she vowed obedience to Church doctrine, she wrote with yearning about

the priesthood: "If I were a priest, how lovingly I would carry you [Christ in the Eucharist] in my hands when you came down from heaven at my call; how lovingly I would bestow you onto people's souls. I want to enlighten people's minds as the prophets and the doctors did. I feel the call of the Apostles." Therese died at age 24, never, of course, having been ordained. Saint Thérèse of Lisieux, *Story of a Soul*, 95.

4. The Canon Law Society of America, *The Code of Canon Law*.

5. Heinzelmann, *Wir schweigen nicht länger! Frauen äußern sich zum II Vatikanischen Konzil*. Heinzelmann self-published the book because—as the story goes—publishers balked at such a controversial topic. The book is incredibly difficult to locate, thus my knowledge comes from secondary sources. The story of Ida Raming and Iris Müller's friendship and collaboration with Heinzelmann can be found online at http://www.ministryforwomen.org/called/heinzelm.asp (accessed December 30, 2014).

6. Two works I have consulted agree on this number of twenty-three: Henold, *Catholic and Feminist*, 46; and Bonavoglia, *Good Catholic Girls*, 24–25. Ruth Wallace alters the number just slightly to twenty-two: Wallace, *They Call Her Pastor*, 2–3.

7. The story of the British economist Barbara Ward proves illustrative here: Ward, an economist and devout Catholic, was invited to report to the Council audience on poverty and sustainable development. When the time came to deliver her remarks, a layman stepped in to present her research to the convened clergy. Briggs, *Double Crossed*, 72–73. Although both laymen and laywomen attending the Council bore the distinction of "auditor," women could not address the Council Fathers, while men could. In her essay in the present volume, Catherine Clifford mentions the laymen Jean Guitton and Patrick Keegan speaking to the assembled bishops.

8. See Clifford in this volume, "The Exercise of Ecclesial Authority in Light of Vatican II" (this volume), 61–62.

9. For more on Tobin's experiences, see Briggs, *Double Crossed*, 72; and McEnroy, *Guests in Their Own House*.

10. For an excellent study on social activism by Catholic women during a different historical moment, see Cummings, *New Women of the Old Faith*. For a thorough history of twentieth-century American Catholic feminism, see Henold, *Catholic and Feminist*.

11. O'Malley, *What Happened at Vatican II*; Faggioli, *Vatican II: The Battle for Meaning*; Gaillardetz and Clifford, *Keys to the Council*; Pope Benedict XVI, *Theological Highlights of Vatican II*; Tanner, *Vatican II: The Essential Texts*; Madges and Daley, *Vatican II: Fifty Personal Stories*.

12. Wilkins, "From Peritus to Pope," 17, 19. Wilkins concludes that Ratzinger moved from supporting to fearing conciliar reforms because of a 1968 student revolt at the German university where he was then teaching. The progressive students' newfound theology of the cross horrified Ratzinger, and he came to see "very close spiritual links" between "the revolutionary interpretation of the council and the political excitement of 1968." Thus, for Wilkins, a disorienting personal experience led Ratzinger to reconsider his position on Vatican II—and more specifically (and pertinent to this essay), his *interpretations* of Vatican II.

13. Komonchak, "Novelty in Continuity." Komonchak also offers a valuable reflection on historical approaches to the Council: "From the standpoints of sociology and

of history, one looks at the council against a broader backdrop, and one cannot limit oneself to the intentions of the popes and bishops or to the final texts. One now studies the impact of the council as experienced, as observed and as implemented."

14. Terms like "conservative," "traditional," "liberal," "progressive," and "feminist" are admittedly imperfect adjectives describing contemporary Catholics. While these words can obscure significant details, they allow for tidy generalizations and convey a kind of essence and motivation, making them useful for projects such as mine here—especially when Vatican II is often thought of as the moment when American Catholicism split into liberal and conservative camps.

15. Komonchak, "Novelty in Continuity."

16. Tentler, "The American Reception and Legacy of the Second Vatican Council" (this volume), 48–56.

17. Martin, *Sex and the Single Savior*, 1.

18. Ibid., 4.

19. Note that, like *Pacem in Terris*, *Gaudium et Spes* also talks at length about conscience. In addition to *Pacem in Terris*'s emphasis on conscience, activist groups have underscored the encyclical's statement that persons can choose their state in life: "Human beings have also the right to choose for themselves the kind of life which appeals to them: whether it is to found a family—in the founding of which both the man and the woman enjoy equal rights and duties—or to embrace the priesthood or the religious life." Pope John XXIII, *Pacem in Terris*. It should come as no surprise that Catholic feminists—in the 1970s as today—cite following their conscience as God's law, over and above the Roman Catholic patriarchy's manmade laws, such as those barring women's ordination. *Pacem in Terris*, RCWP would argue, has made personal conscience foundational. Thus, the group frequently makes reference to conscience in describing and defending its actions. Meehan, Doku, and Rue, "A Brief Overview of Womenpriests."

20. Vatican Council II, *Gaudium et Spes*. *Gaudium et Spes* was issued in Latin, and a number of translations exist. The translations I cite here come from the Vatican website, and thus I retain the masculine language.

21. Vatican Council II, *Gaudium et Spes*, 29.

22. Ibid., 55.

23. Halter, *The Papal 'No,'* 6, 22, 24. Briggs, *Double Crossed*, 44–46. Of course, some women pursued theology anyway. The feminist theologian Mary Daly, for her part, though born and raised in New York State, attained two doctorates in sacred theology and philosophy from a university in Switzerland, as no American program would accept her for theology.

24. *Gaudium et Spes* offered, "Furthermore, it is to be hoped that many of the laity will receive a sufficient formation in the sacred sciences and that some will dedicate themselves professionally to these studies, developing and deepening them by their own labors. In order that they may fulfill their function, let it be recognized that all the faithful, whether clerics or laity, possess a lawful freedom of inquiry, freedom of thought and of expressing their mind with humility and fortitude in those matters on which they enjoy competence." *Gaudium et Spes*, 62.

25. Henold, *Catholic and Feminist*, 21.

26. Women's Ordination Conference, "Our Story." For a vivid picture of Catholic life in Detroit under Archbishop Dearden (1958–80), see Tentler's essay "The American Reception and Legacy of the Second Vatican Council" in this volume.

27. Gardiner, *Women and Catholic Priesthood.*

28. Women's Ordination Conference, "Top Ten Reasons to Ordain Women."

29. Women Can Be Priests, homepage, http://www.womenpriests.org (accessed December 30, 2014). The quotation is cited as being from *Gaudium et Spes*, 62; *Canon Law*, no. 212, para. 3. Notably, the website's authors show that this "freedom of inquiry" is echoed in *Gaudium et Spes* as well as in Canon Law. Womenpriests.org, founded by John Wijngaards, is a group of theologians seeking continued discussion about women's ordination.

30. Call to Action, "Vatican II: Church Forward," also supports women's ordination. The group does not offer a citation for the John XXIII quote, but a quick web search found the quote on Vatican II: The Voice of the Church, "The Church's English Voice—Bishop Christopher Butler, OSB," http://vatican2voice.org/4basics/papal.htm (accessed December 30, 2014), where it is attributed to the Vatican archive. It is also quoted on the cover of Hebblethwaite, *John XXIII, Pope of the Council.*

31. Significantly, the Vatican never made the commission's findings public. Information on the Pontifical Biblical Commission came to light only because it was leaked, and thus the commission's findings are covered primarily in books advocating women's ordination—and not in texts working apologetically on the Church's behalf. See L. Swidler and A. Swidler, *Women Priests*; Halter, *The Papal 'No,'* 37–41.

32. Congregation for the Doctrine of the Faith, *Inter Insigniores*, http://www .papalencyclicals.net/Paul06/p6interi.htm (accessed December 30, 2014).

33. Pope John Paul II, *Ordinatio Sacerdotalis*, para. 4. Scholars have debated whether this was the pope's way of claiming infallibility without speaking ex cathedra, which in the past had been the formal way of citing infallible doctrine. For a discussion of the document, as well as a summary of scholarly discussion about the document's potentially infallible nature, see Halter, *The Papal 'No,'* 94–107.

34. Raming, "Situation of Women in the Roman Catholic Church," 21–26; Müller, "My Story, Condensed," 19–20; Ida Raming, e-mail interview with author, January 9, 2011.

35. The ordained women were Pia Brunner, Gisela Forster, Iris Müller, and Ida Raming of Germany; Christine Mayr-Lumetzberger and Adelinde Theresia Roitinger of Austria; and Angela White (a pseudonym for the Austrian-born Dagmar Celeste) of the United States. To be sure, this movement started in Europe, growing out of the cooperation between American and European women, through WOC and also WOW (Women's Ordination Worldwide). For more on the Danube Seven and the first RCWP ordination, see Allen, "Ordinations Ignite Debate over Tactics"; Allen, "Seven Women 'Ordained' Priests June 29"; Forster, "The Start"; Mayr-Lumetzberger, "Reflections on My Way"; Müller, "My Story, Condensed"; Raming, "Situation of Women in the Roman Catholic Church"; Celeste, "Soli Deo Amor."

36. Forster, "The Start"; McGrath, "The Road Less Traveled By."

37. In Roman Catholicism, excommunication is a penalty designed to encourage censured individuals to rebuild their relationship with the Church. Excommunication

is not intended to forever remove someone from the Church; rather, excommunicants are still expected to attend Mass, though they cannot participate in a ministerial capacity or receive the sacraments. Types of excommunication are *latae sententiae*, or automatic, and *ferendae sententiae*, imposed by Church authority. To date, all of RCWP's ordained are excommunicated *latae sententiae*. Note, the Danube Seven were excommunicated *ferendae sententiae*; three women associated with a 2007 ordination in St. Louis, Missouri, were also excommunicated by formal decree (see Burke and Breier, "Declaration of Excommunication of Patricia Fresen, Rose Hudson, and Elsie McGrath").

38. Roman Catholic Womenpriests, "RCWP FAQs."

39. Roman Catholic Womenpriests—North America, "Vision Statement." A video from the same year introducing viewers to the RCWP shows the then public relations director Bridget Mary Meehan echoing this sentiment from the Vision Statement: "Roman Catholic Womenpriests: Vision and Mission," August 29, 2007, video clip, YouTube, http://www.youtube.com/watch?v=cJrn-rmHpPQ.

40. Meehan, "Roman Catholic Women Priests Invite You to Stand With Fr. Roy Bourgeois to Resist Vatican Oppression and to Proclaim Equality for Women in the Church."

41. Roman Catholic Womenpriests, "RCWP Call on Pope to Lift Excommunications."

42. Roman Catholic Womenpriests, "Roman Catholic Womenpriests' Response to Vatican Decrees of Excommunication." Ratzinger's commentary was found in Vorgrimler, *Commentary on the Documents of Vatican II*, 5: 134.

43. RCWP has a range of arguments explaining and advocating its position, many of which do not connect specifically to Vatican II and thus stand outside this essay's scope. Three examples are worth mentioning here: 1) The group often cites Galatians 3:28 as an example of early Christians' egalitarian aims: "There is no longer Jew or Greek, there is no longer slave or free, there is no longer male and female; for all of you are one in Christ Jesus." 2) RCWP compares the group's efforts with the struggles for justice associated with both the American civil rights movement and the South African struggle against apartheid; see Patricia Fresen, "Prophetic Obedience: The Experience and Vision of Roman Catholic Womenpriests" (speech given at the Southeast Pennsylvania Women's Ordination Conference, March 2005). 3) RCWP's women also argue that the clergy sex-abuse crisis could have been avoided had women been part of the priesthood. See Bayly, "'We Are All the Rock.'"

44. Tentler, "The American Reception and Legacy of the Second Vatican Council" (this volume), 39.

5

# QUEBEC'S WAYSIDE CROSSES AND THE CREATION OF CONTEMPORARY DEVOTIONALISM

*Hillary Kaell*

"To a stranger's eyes, Québec often seems like a land literally colonized by Heaven."
—Jean Simard, *Le Québec pour terrain: Itinéraire d'un missionnaire du patrimoine religieux*, 13

Look at a road map or drive Quebec's byways and sacred markers are everywhere: saints' names grace nearly every town and village, Catholic churches punctuate horizons and skylines, and three thousand *croix de chemin* rise up at regular intervals along rural roads. These wayside crosses are made of wood or iron, usually painted white, and can be simple or elaborately decorated. Each one is about sixteen to twenty-five feet tall and must be visible to passersby. A wayside cross is always blessed by a priest at construction.

Quebecers popularly associate the crosses with a distant past, beginning with the sixteenth-century explorer Jacques Cartier.[1] Yet in their current form, the crosses more accurately date to the latter part of the Marian century, from the 1870s to the 1950s. Construction peaked between 1945 and 1955, especially during the Jubilee and Marian years of 1950 and 1954, when priests actively promoted it.[2] Vatican II and the so-called Quiet Revolution, a period of rapid sociopolitical secularization and modernization, changed wayside cross devotion significantly. Scholars took note and, from 1972 to 1979, a dozen researchers in Quebec undertook a government-funded survey. For the project's leader, the ethnologist Jean Simard, the wayside cross was a "despised heritage" caught between iconoclasts of the Quiet Revolution and Catholic conciliar reformists. It seemed fated to disappear as modernity advanced.[3]

In the 1980s, local newspapers, radio and television specials picked up the story and eulogized the crosses further. A 1986 poem written by a housewife, Camille des Ormes, and reproduced in a local history book, evokes the prevailing sentiment: "They were numerous once, these *croix du chemin* . . . / It was a sign of faith, from the people who came from France . . . / Today, we have forgotten these *croix du chemin* / Like a wounded being, they attract pity."[4]

Though the popular narrative is often a romanticized lament, while the scholarly one viewed as inevitable (or celebrated) Quebec's progressive secularization, both fundamentally agree on one major point: the crosses are ignored and forgotten, a remnant of a time now past. This assumption pervades discussions about post-1960s Quebec Catholicism more broadly, discussions that focus on decline, secularism, and "the crumbling of tradition."[5]

Without minimizing the changes that have occurred in Quebec Catholicism, I propose that we reverse the approach. Rather than dwell on how many crosses have disappeared, we might fruitfully ask why so many crosses are, in fact, being maintained and restored. For even as Simard wrote of the "despised tradition" and Camille des Ormes penned her lament, wayside crosses were going up around the province.[6] In the 1970s, the yearly rate of construction, though lower than at its peak in the 1950s, was comparable to that in the 1930s. Since then, the number of crosses has stayed constant, in part because of sturdier building techniques (metal instead of wood), but largely because those that fall down are replaced. Most of the parishes I surveyed sustained about a 20 percent loss since the 1970s; put differently, eight out of ten crosses still stand.[7]

This essay relies on archival sources, a telephone survey of two hundred parishes with crosses, and a set of fifty conversational interviews with cross caretakers—the individuals who look after the crosses today.[8] My aim here is twofold. Scholarship on the wayside crosses, and on contemporary Catholicism in Quebec, has largely focused on sociological surveys of decline or modes of governance (*laïcité*). Studies of Vatican II center on negotiations between Quebecois clerical and lay elites. Little work in either vein examines contemporary lived Catholicism and the local reception of Vatican II reforms.[9] Inspired by the recent interest in these topics among scholars of U.S. Catholic studies, my first aim, then, is to use the crosses as a lens to examine grassroots Catholicism in (mainly) rural Quebec.[10] The result will provide a more nuanced portrait of a province where church attendance is now the lowest in North America yet 92 percent of French Canadians still identify as Catholics, 91 percent baptize their children, and 30 percent say daily prayers.[11]

I also draw on the Quebec case to explore the role of devotions in contemporary Catholicism. These external affective practices include the novena, the rosary, the Stations of the Cross and, in Quebec, the month of Mary prayers and outdoor benedictions—all associated with the wayside crosses. Evaluating the Council's impact, scholars have described the precipitous decline of these and other devotions. Priests stopped promoting what they had earlier championed, including *croix de chemin* construction.[12] Simard is thus correct when he notes that the crosses were, in many ways, out of step with Church reforms. Yet as we complicate the rupture-continuity paradigm in studies of Vatican II, we should also reevaluate the assumption that devotions thrived before the Council and then fell into irreversible decline. Once supposedly traditional devotions, like the crosses, are viewed as in flux and changing, we can begin to ask how they may have taken on new meanings, even becoming potent symbols of modern Catholicism. It is the reason that wayside crosses are flourishing today.

## A Short History of Quebec and Its Crosses

In 1608, French colonists founded the city of Quebec. In 1759, England defeated France and, four years later, formally took control of the territory. Throughout the following generation, Quebec elites began to articulate a more self-conscious platform for French Canadian survival, with Catholicism as the central axis ensuring their distinctiveness and national mission in the world. Though never an established church, Catholicism (especially in rural areas) was fully imbricated in civil society—in healthcare, education, and local politics—providing an institutional counterpoint to the Anglo-Protestant control of macro affairs such as the federal parliament, army, and economy.[13]

By the early twentieth century, priests like Lionel Groulx and organizations like Montreal's Société Saint-Jean-Baptiste were actively constructing and promoting a Quebec identity rooted in a romantic vision of the peasant farmer—simple, unchanging, and Catholic.[14] When these intellectuals first noted the wayside crosses in an 1896 issue of the *Bulletin des recherches historiques*, the wooden constructions seemed the perfect encapsulation of this religious-nationalist ethos.[15] In 1915, the Société Saint-Jean-Baptiste sponsored a competition of fictional stories extolling the crosses, later reprinted as a popular book. In the 1920s, a lifelong member of the society, the Montreal lawyer Édouard-Zotique Massicotte, took up the crosses' cause, conducting a photographic survey and promoting their importance for French Canadian identity and Anglo-American motor tourism, a growing source of revenue at the time.[16] During the following decades, wayside crosses invariably came to be portrayed, as one magazine article put it in 1943, as proof of how rural people "have so well conserved the precious

Canadian painter Horatio Walker immortalized the wayside cross in *De Profundis* (1916). His image of simple Quebecois farmers stopped in prayer epitomizes the romanticism of this period. (© National Gallery of Canada, Ottawa)

heritage of faith, bequeathed by their ancestors."[17] Even as constructions peaked in the 1940s and 1950s, elite commentators associated the crosses with an idealized, Catholic past.[18]

Though Quebecois promoters generally associated *croix de chemin* with Brittany, a region of France tied to the French Canadian national myth of origin, wayside crosses were actually widespread across Catholic Europe.[19] Popularized after the thirteenth century, they were made of stone, wood, or iron, often with carved embellishments. After the fifteenth century, crosses began to include representations of Jesus's crucified body and scenes from the Passion. Gentry, clergy, or religious orders hired professional artisans to create these elaborate crosses, for varied reasons. They could be commemorative, supplicatory, or penitential, and thus a method of gaining indulgences.[20] Wayside crosses delimited physical boundaries between towns and properties, marked out sacred places, mapped the routes to pilgrimage shrines, offered protection against evil spirits, and gave asylum for convicts. Because the open road was a recognized allegory for the soul's journey, the crosses were portrayed as salvific anchors reminding Christians not to stray from a godly path. Travelers regularly halted their journeys there to pray.[21]

Once transplanted to Canada, aspects of the devotion secondary in Europe seem to have gained new prominence. I focus for a moment on the time between the 1870s and 1950s, the period culminating in the construction boom noted above. In this era, crosses were built for three main reasons in Quebec: to commemorate an event, usually the founding of a parish or school; by a single family or individual to fulfill a vow and secure future protection against disease, untimely death, forest fires, drought, and agricultural pests; by the families of a *rang* (a rural grouping of houses) as a gathering place if the parish church was too far for regular visits. The first two reasons clearly originate in Europe, though they may have proven more central in Quebec. The third seems particular to the New World, with its widely dispersed agricultural settlements. While Europe's crosses marked distant roads to pilgrimage shrines, Quebec's crosses were understood primarily as local gathering places and thus rarely planted far from people's homes.[22]

In devotional terms, Quebec's crosses served one major purpose: during May—the month of Mary—residents of a *rang* gathered there to pray a novena, say the rosary, and sometimes hold Mass, if a priest was available.[23] These group prayers, which focused on planting and the harvest, show how closely the Quebec wayside cross was intertwined with agriculture; according to surveys in the 1970s, 80 percent of *croix de chemin* prayers and vows concerned the land. The connection to Mary thus likely stems from her long association in popular Catholic devotion with springtime, signifying new life. More immediately, May as "Mary's Month" was promoted widely in nineteenth-century North America, one of many monthly devotions at the time.[24]

Aesthetically, Quebec crosses are often distinguishable from European ones because they are painted white, staked close to the ground (not set on a high column or plinth), and encircled with a garden. They often include the *arma Christi* (instruments of the Passion), iconography that dates back to the ninth century. Especially popular are the ladder and the lance, the *titulus crucis*, a stylized heart, a rooster, and a sun or a circle (likely adapted from the crown of thorns).[25] Jesus's body usually remains absent. This pattern seems to have no precedent in Europe, where crosses (and iconography of *arma Christi* generally) include the crucified body, the Man of Sorrows, or Veronica's Veil. In Quebec, the absent Christ probably has practical origins. With wood serving as the primary building material, finely detailed carvings could be destroyed in a season in the region's harsh climate. Most nineteenth- and twentieth-century Quebecois villagers also lacked the skill to depict the human form. In Europe, elites or religious orders often commissioned crosses and hired professional artisans to carve them.[26]

Yet one should be careful with generalizations. Quebec crosses have always been objects in flux. Years after construction, if a builder or a wealthy villager could, he might add a sculpture of Jesus's body—which became easier to acquire once a Montreal-based distributer began to import European-made religious statues in the 1920s.[27] If a parish could afford a corpus, it was usually purchased for the cemetery; a fair number of wayside crosses adorned with the body today received it when the cemetery statue was replaced. Styles also change. Sacred Heart devotion, popular in Quebec at the time when many crosses were first built, undoubtedly gave rise to the most widespread decorative feature—a stylized heart. Yet today's caretakers rarely make the connection; the Sacred Heart is less popular, and the now simplified *croix de chemin* heart bears little resemblance to it.

A cross's decorative elements—such as the heart or a saint statue if there is a niche—seem to have been chosen mainly for aesthetic reasons and based on the availability of prefabricated statues. Including a Saint Anthony, for example, did not mean that prayers were directed to him.[28] Nor were Quebec's crosses as strongly associated with Jesus's suffering and redemptive death as in Europe. Perhaps this meaning faded because the Passion was not depicted graphically, or vice versa. Whatever the case, Quebec crosses were associated primarily with *le Seigneur* (the Father) and his protection against natural scourges, ill health, and untimely death. Though people

Ornamented cross in Ange-Gardien village. Erected in 1988, it is a close replica of the first one from 1952. The lance, ladder, sponge, nails, crown of thorns, and rooster (on top) are popular symbols of the Passion. (Photo by Monique Bellemare, 2010)

A wayside cross on the road leading out of the village of Saint-Roch-de-l'Achigan. The corpus was donated by the cemetery when its caretakers bought a new one. (Author's collection, 2013)

A wayside cross (left) outside the town of Marieville. A local man built the wooden cross in 1999. In 2011 it was replaced with a similar one (right), now made of sturdy metal. (Photos by Monique Bellemare, 2010 and 2013)

may have favored Mary and Jesus at home or in church, at the wayside cross these divine persons clearly served as intermediaries with the Father. Supplications acknowledged human sin generally (we sin and beg God's mercy) but, unlike in Europe, the Quebec wayside cross rarely had associations with personal sin or penance, and never with indulgences.[29]

## (Re)constructions on the Ground

Wayside cross devotion changed significantly after the Quiet Revolution (1960–66), during which time Quebec urbanized, secularized, and set up state-run institutions at breathtaking speed. Rates of church attendance and fertility plummeted.[30] It is important to note, however, that the impact of these reforms was by no means as sudden as is often portrayed, nor were they consistent throughout the province. Catholicism has retained significantly more importance in rural areas than in urban ones. According to my survey, 97 percent of cross caretakers describe themselves as "believing" Catholics; 83 percent are also "practicing," meaning that they go to church at least once a month. This level of commitment, more common in rural villages and towns, is atypical for Quebec as a whole, where monthly Mass attendance lies at just 20 percent.[31]

In the 1960s and 1970s, the crosses were affected by increased religious apathy and changing religious styles (the novena, for example, was no longer *en vogue*). More proximate causes of decline resulted from the state-led modernization of transportation and schools. Wayside crosses lessened in importance as rural people purchased cars and could make regular trips to the parish church. More traffic also meant more motor accidents, felling crosses that were never replaced; many others were knocked down as authorities widened, paved, and rerouted rural roads in a major infrastructure campaign. Less dramatic but equally devastating, in the mid-1960s village schools were replaced by centralized ones run by new *commissions scolaires* (boards of education). The loss of local control constituted the first step in deconfessionalizing public schools and, more immediately, meant the loss of rural school mistresses, who had often organized month of Mary prayers.[32]

After this low point, a wave of reconstructions began in the mid-1980s. They continue today. Three short vignettes illustrate how such projects often come about. Pierette Malo, for example, lives in the countryside near Joliette, a city of twenty thousand. Because she grew up in the city, she was unaware of the crosses as a child. Yet in 1992, at age fifty-two, she and her husband built a cross in front of their house. They had been planning it for a while. "In our travels [around Quebec], we stopped often at beautiful *croix de chemin* to pray," she says, "and we said if we can one day—because it takes some money—we'll put up a cross on our land for people to pray." Pierette and her husband hired a local craftsman who built it according to their design—with decorative sun rays and a Sacred Heart (because they live in Sacred Heart parish). During the 1990s, she painted it regularly and tended flowers at its base, helped by her neighbors. She also held gatherings there twice a year for people to pray the rosary together. In 2000, she and her husband sold the property to move closer to health services in town. The new owners do not look after the cross as Pierette did, but she still stops there to pray when passing by.

Guy Laverdière, seventy, has always lived on the same road outside Saint-Lazare-de-Bellechasse, a village of just over a thousand people. In 1941, a local man erected a wayside cross to fulfill a vow he had made when his daughter was ill. Guy is not related to the original owner, who has long since died, but he passes the cross every day, since it stands only half a mile from his house. Through this daily contact, he says, he grew to love the cross and always gave it a *salut* (a gesture of respect). When the cross showed signs of wear in 1974, Guy rebuilt it, and again in 1997. In 2003, he decided to replace the wooden cross with iron. Because of significant expenses, he asked his neighbors to contribute, which they readily did. Now, he says proudly, "even when I die, it'll stay up for a good long while." He is careful to note that, although he does most of the maintenance, everyone in the *rang* sees the cross as owned communally. In recent years, the women on the parish committee have reinstituted month of Mary prayers, which Guy sometimes attends.

The sixty-three-year-old Michel Pomerleau provides a final example. He is the Grand Chevalier (Grand Knight) of the Knights of Columbus in Saint-Côme-Linière, a rural town of two thousand people. In 2011, a recently widowed woman approached him and asked for help painting the cross on her land. He agreed since it seemed like a small job and was consistent with the Knights' mission to help the widowed and the orphaned. Once his group of volunteers arrived, they saw that the cross's cement base also needed repair. So they stayed and did that too. "No one [in our council] decided to work on the crosses specifically," Michel says, "but then it just turned out—the woman thanked us when we were done—and we said, you know there's another cross in the village behind Paquet grocery and no one can see it. That doesn't make any sense! So the whole gang, we went down there and got to it." Local businesses donated the materials and people have begun to request that Michel help them restore the crosses in their *rangs* too. Each restoration is followed by a benediction from the parish priest, a ceremony that has drawn about fifty people each time. Michel now hopes to redo all fourteen crosses in his parish at a rate of two per year.

## Factors Driving Contemporary Constructions

The stories of Pierette, Guy, and Michel illustrate a few key trends. According to my survey, about 33 percent of crosses standing today were restored or built in the 1980s, 24 percent in the 1990s, and 30 percent in the 2000s (or 36 percent if we include second restorations of 1980s crosses). Twelve percent have been maintained since the 1960s and needed no reconstruction. Although Quebecers associate the crosses with "the ancestors" in a general sense, only about 10 percent are actually maintained by direct family members of the original builders. Most caretakers—who become a cross's de facto owners—adopt a public cross nearby, as Guy did, or move to a new property and inherit its cross. Other times, a cross belongs to the municipality or parish, and they, or the Knights of Columbus, assume the cost of upkeep.[33] A well-maintained cross nearly always owes its existence to a single individual (or a small group). Without this champion, it is generally forgotten. And once a cross falls, it is rarely replaced.

So what accounts for the restorations? As Quebecois scholars like Simard have acknowledged, the trend defies their earlier predictions.[34] Scholars have credited their own studies with driving local restorations, while heritage professionals view them as a successful example of government intervention.[35] From 2001 to 2003, three government-funded chairs were instituted at francophone universities to study heritage (especially religious heritage), and there have been a number of affiliated conferences, publications, and TV specials on Télé-Québec.[36] Since 1995, the Quebec government has spent more than $270 million on the maintenance and restoration of Catholic buildings. Its Council for Religious Heritage has a budget of $14 million a year, more than any other Canadian province.[37]

This activity signals a new approach to understanding Catholicism in Quebec. For heritage professionals, and the scholars allied with them, government support of Catholic objects and rituals ("immaterial heritage") forms part of a process of *patrimonialisation*, where religious objects become the cultural heritage of a people. In this view, modernity inevitably diminishes the religious meaning of an object, which nevertheless retains importance in fostering a distinct national identity.[38] As a result, ecclesiastical authorities who close churches and amalgamate parishes may be blamed for destroying a religious heritage that, for heritage professionals, is no longer the property of the Church at all, but part of a communal secular identity.[39]

While at a diffuse cultural level the *patrimonialisation* of Catholicism has affected cross caretakers, as I describe below, its direct impact is negligible. Very few caretakers are aware of academic work on the crosses or know about government grants to develop local tourism.[40] These factors may have an indirect impact in how they are filtered through "local experts," however, people who since the 1990s have benefited from provincial grants to set up regional historical societies. These societies restore few crosses themselves, but the media they produce about wayside crosses (booklets, pamphlets, and educational events) may foster local pride and thereby encourage reconstructions, though caretakers rarely cite this influence directly.[41]

According to caretakers, a few major factors drive the restorations. One is increased motor travel. There is some irony here; after all, the growth of car traffic and transportation infrastructure felled many crosses in the 1960s and 1970s. Yet it also meant that Quebecers could see large swathes of their own province with new ease. Caretakers describe being inspired to restore their crosses after seeing well-maintained crosses in other regions. In Pierette's case, a city girl got to know a rural phenomenon and adopted it as her own, even building a brand-new cross.

A second motivating factor overlaps with the first: building a wayside cross has always been a way to accrue social capital (a topic assiduously avoided in the often romanticized popular literature about the crosses). Today, caretakers joke that rural people undertake restorations because if one *rang* or village does it, everyone else wants to "one up them." If the original builder is known, the cross also retains his name ("the Cormier cross") and ensures his family's place in the local landscape. A rural cross constitutes a directional point and an orienting device: "Pass by the Cormier cross and take a right"; "Wait for me at the cross"; "It's snowing so hard you can't see the cross."[42] At a more personal level, restoring or building a cross may elevate a person to a local celebrity for a time.

Marielle Lemay, a seventy-year-old caretaker who built a cross with her husband in 2007, notes the gratification it can provide. She grew up on the seventh *rang* of her village. Fifty years ago when she married, she moved down the road to the tenth *rang*, where there was no wayside cross. Years later, to coincide with the parish's 175th anniversary, she decided to put one up in front of her house. While municipalities or parishes often see such occasions as the impetus to restore their crosses, individuals like Marielle tend to downplay these particular events, even if they also refer to them.[43] She would have built the cross regardless, she insists, once her road began to attract more traffic. She describes what it means to her today: "I'm proud of the good thing [*bon coup*] we did. It's not arrogant pride [*orgueil*], just pride [*fierté*] that I participated in a sense of unity and did something for the people here. . . .[The cross] symbolizes our belonging in the Catholic faith."

Caretakers distinguish between *orgueil* and *fierté*. While in English both words translate to "pride," in French *orgueil* connotes sinful self-importance. Caretakers of new (or recently restored) crosses position their actions carefully, since they often acquire a central place in community affairs. The first month she and her husband put up their cross, for example, Marielle became hostess to the whole *rang*, serving juice and cookies every night when people came to pray. At its benediction, sixty people came out for a full day of picnicking and games at her house. She was honored at church for her efforts. Today, people still stop at her cross and neighbors thank her regularly. While such praise could go to one's head (*orgueil*), Marielle insists that she feels a healthy pride (*fierté*)—it is a work for others that expresses and promotes a shared Catholic unity.

Another major factor driving current restorations is the growing involvement of the Knights of Columbus, evident in Michel Pomerleau's story above. The Knights are a laymen's fraternal organization that formed in Connecticut in 1882 and came to Quebec at the turn of the century. The organization grew slowly, not least because the U.S. headquarters ignored requests for a French translation of the official charter until 1935. Then, in the 1940s and 1950s, Quebec membership more than doubled, and the provincial council successfully lobbied for its own secretariat and a name change, becoming the Chevaliers de Colomb.[44] The group circulated French-language publications steadily after 1950. The magazine of the Chevaliers, *Le Colombien*, began publication in 1968. Today, the organization counts more than one hundred thousand members across the province.[45]

By the late 1990s, the Chevaliers were restoring crosses throughout the province. The provincial executive and regional Grand Knights, like Michel, tell a common story: individual caretakers approached them for help and they responded as a purely local initiative. Though provincial leaders insist that they at no point expressly encouraged these activities,[46] *Le Colombien* began to feature notices and photos of local restorations between 1984 and 1987, and again in the mid-1990s. In 1997, the executive's new yearly awards program—reported also in the magazine—highlighted the restorations too; during the 2000s, cross restorations regularly received prizes in the Parish Activities category.[47] Some local Chevaliers recall that these photos and the resulting conversations at annual provincial congresses spurred their interest.[48]

Nearly all cross caretakers—including the Chevaliers—are in their fifties or older. Another reason for the surge in restorations may therefore correspond to what the sociologists Michele Dillon and Paul Wink have observed about the North American lifecycle: there are ebbs and flows in religiosity, and "late adulthood" constitutes a high point.[49] Cross caretakers are in good health, often retired, and have more time to devote to parish activities. While they have been lifelong Catholics, at this point faith may become more important, in part because they are thinking about the legacy they will leave. Guy Laverdière is typical when he underlines that, even after he dies, his iron cross will stay up "a good long while." Many caretakers say that it will last "an eternity," a notion sometimes illustrated with dramatic effect. In Saint-Roch-de-l'Achigan village, for example, the local historical society recounts the story of the Mercier cross. In 1924, when Télésphore Mercier and his wife Louise-Marie bought a farm, he built a cross, saying, "A cross, it's made to stay." After Télésphore's death in 1955, Louise-Marie maintained it and saved up to build an iron replacement, which would stay "forever" as he had wanted. She erected the new cross in 1974 and, the very day after it went up, was hit by a car and killed right in front of it. "Mission accomplished," the local historians conclude without a trace of irony. The metal cross still stands today, maintained by one of Louise-Marie's sons.[50]

Because contemporary families have fewer children, and because most sons no longer stay on the land, caretakers must ensure permanence in new ways. The issue constitutes a major question as aging caretakers sell their property to move closer to towns with better amenities for the elderly. Thus Pierette and her husband had to leave their cross behind. The widow who approached Michel Pomerleau had a cross that she could no longer physically maintain. The result seems to be a twofold shift. First, much to heritage experts' chagrin, caretakers are adopting sturdier building materials: iron, vinyl siding, car paint, and stainless-steel screws require fewer repairs and last a long time. A second shift may place the responsibility for crosses outside the traditional domains of family and *rang*, without moving entirely beyond the local. Increasingly, lay organizations, like the Chevaliers, or smaller groups of independent citizens take over a cross when its owners ask for help.

A final reason for the restorations deserves mention, especially since caretakers highlight it most: simply, the cross *needed* it. In their telling, a cross's own material need spurs human activity. A wooden cross must be repaired regularly and usually replaced within about twenty-five to thirty-five years.[51] If cross construction was at a high point from circa 1945 to 1955, major restorations became necessary in the 1980s. In this case, caretakers stepped into a role they saw as natural. A blessed cross is a religious object, they insist, and it must be maintained.[52]

Public Space, Private Devotion

While these explanations help clarify why restorations are on the rise right now, they only scratch the surface of what the crosses mean to the people involved. Why perpetuate a devotion that seems out of step with Vatican II reforms? Why maintain a large, public cross in a province where Catholicism is so often viewed as antimodern and retrograde?[53] The answer lies in the fact that Catholic devotions are not static and unchanging; today's restorers view the crosses very differently from their parents.

Typical of Quebecers more widely, caretakers support religious reforms since Vatican II. When they compare their childhoods and today, they applaud what they see as a new ethic toward voluntary participation in institutional Catholicism. One used to be obliged to go to Mass and confession, they say, without feeling properly spiritual and contrite. Otherwise the neighbors would talk. Monthly Mass attendance has fallen dramatically—from more than 80 percent in the mid-1960s to 20 percent today—but caretakers insist that Catholicism has, in some ways, benefited from a quality-over-quantity approach.[54] "Today, on the other hand," says Marielle Lemay, "when you go to church or to the *croix de chemin*, it's more out of actual reflection, out of conviction." Andrée Clouatre, a sixty-seven-year-old caretaker, agrees: "Before people weren't more believing than now. They just followed. They went to church, that's it. People who participate now are *actually* participating, not in name only."

The emphasis on sincere participation reflects the shift since Vatican II toward a theology of the people of God, a vision of the Church articulated most clearly in *Lumen Gentium*. In one way, it is not surprising that caretakers associate the wayside crosses with this idea. The crosses have always occupied an interstitial place between the institutional Church and extraliturgical practice: priests were necessary for major occasions like the initial benediction, but laypeople organized and led the devotions; crosses were associated with official prayers (like the rosary), but they stood out in the open and often far away from the parish church. However, while some scholars have argued that the crosses were therefore never really "Catholic" at all (and thus more valuable as indigenous Quebec folklore), most caretakers disagree.[55] They are practicing Catholics; for them, the crosses reflect the Church's new theology and have evolved alongside it.

These changes become evident in the types of prayers they say and the persons to whom they are addressed. As noted, wayside crosses were traditionally associated with vows for protection against a variety of natural scourges related to health and agriculture. Today, caretakers dismiss such vows as akin to superstition. According to Pierette, people used to think, "You're going to say a prayer and it will be better: my mother is sick with cancer, so I'll say a prayer—poof!—she'll be healed. No, it's not like that. Now it is more, please give me the strength to get through it. It's not the same thing at all." The only vows associated with the crosses today are those for help during personal health crises or accidents, which were rare a generation ago.[56]

Mid-twentieth-century crosses were once associated with *rangs* or villages with a particular devotion to the Virgin.[57] The act of standing at the cross imploring God's mercy mirrored Mary's dolorous vigil at Calvary, and villagers addressed their prayers to her so she would intercede with the Father.[58] Today, caretakers almost uniformly associate the crosses with Jesus, though they may still pray the rosary on occasion. Michel Pomerleau describes the cross's symbolism in three interlocking parts: "[It says] that we are practicing [and], secondly, that we are Christians. And it's for us to say Jesus died for us on the cross." Although many caretakers recognize the Passion as important, they do not meditate on Jesus's suffering body (when it is depicted on the crosses, it is usually a muted white; see the Saint-Roch-de-l'Achigan cross, shown above). They focus instead on Jesus's love for humankind. Pierette, like many caretakers, used her cross as an object lesson to help her grandson develop a relationship with Jesus: "When he was [young], we would go to the cross and wave and he'd say, 'Bonjour Jésus!' That's how you show them."

For caretakers, this emphasis on the wayside cross as fundamentally related to an individual's relationship with God and Jesus is key as they reposition the devotion within contemporary Catholicism. They say variously, "It's more personal, it's less about lots of meeting together. It's more person-to-person or, you know, person-to-God"; or, "When I was young, it was a place for the people of the *rang* or the village to gather. . . . Today, it's a sign that there are still believers in the world, in our current reality."[59] Communal prayers during the month of Mary, once central to wayside cross devotionalism, are now downplayed or deemed irrelevant. They typify the obligatory social events and practices that, for caretakers (and Quebecers generally), are the hallmark of pre-1960s Catholicism.[60]

Once the wayside cross is reenvisioned as symbolic of an individual's relationship with God, and distanced from societal relationships, it also becomes potentially less problematic in contemporary Quebec. Civil society reforms have chipped away at Catholicism's once overwhelming public presence. Catechism was taken out of regular public school curricula in the mid-1990s, for example, and there are regular discussions in the media about the possibility of a French-style *laïcité* that bans personal religious signs (e.g., a crucifix necklace, a kippah, or the hijab) in public places. Caretakers blame these changes variously on a militantly secularist minority and on immigrant others (Muslims primarily) who they believe are trying to impose their beliefs and suppress Catholic ones.[61] Yet at no point do they express a desire to return to a pre-1960s Quebec, which they see as incompatible with fostering the individual conscience necessary for a more sincere, voluntary Catholicism. More pragmatically, they have also had to accept that many of their neighbors and children are no longer practicing Catholics.

Caretakers respond to this fact in a few overlapping ways. First, as noted, they emphasize that wayside cross devotion no longer publically imposes Catholicism but aids a personal relationship with God. Second, they restore older crosses. Nearly 79 percent of crosses today are restorations, compared to only 27 percent in the mid-1970s.[62] Restoring an old cross is in keeping with the broader cultural impetus toward heritage preservation and thus may prove more palatable to non-practicing friends and family. Jean-Marc Thouin, sixty-four, has restored five crosses in the past decade as the Grand Chevalier in the village of Saint-Jovite. "I would've liked to have one on my property," he admits, "but I decided— today, there are a lot people even in my family who aren't necessarily practicing Catholics—so I decided to concentrate on the existing [historical] crosses rather than put [a new] one up. Some of my family wouldn't want it in front of the house."

Mainly, however, caretakers restore old crosses because they, like most Quebecers since the 1990s, have come to see historical objects as a way of promoting and reinforcing a national *patrimoine*. Since 1998, the Chevaliers' magazine has urged its readers to restore crosses using this language, echoing government heritage professionals. Because no easy separation exists in Quebec between identity and Catholicism, caretakers make no attempt to distinguish between levels of belonging: for them, the cross connects passersby simultaneously to Catholicism, to God, to the ancestors, and to Quebec identity. If their neighbors value the cross as secular history, caretakers underline that precisely these multiple meanings let wayside crosses retain their importance for the community as a whole.

Last, and most important, caretakers deny that most Quebecers are truly secular. They acknowledge dismal rates of institutional participation but, like other North American Catholics, no longer view Mass attendance as the best indication of belief.[63] They attribute the decline to what they see as outside factors, unrelated to people's relationship with God: the unhealthy pace of modern life in dual-income families, the impact of the sex abuse scandals, and the Church's stance against female ordination. They see these as institutional or societal failures, but they nevertheless remain optimistic about Catholicism. "People are still Catholic," says Guy Laverdière firmly. "They might not go to Mass, but they're Catholics just the same." Pierette Malo adds: "Today there are a lot of non-practicing people because they aren't obliged to go (to Mass). But when you speak to people, often, often they talk about faith. They don't realize it, but they have it still. It's different, but it's still faith. Many young couples absolutely want their children baptized. They are non-practicing but there is still that spark of faith."

For caretakers, the main proof of young people's continuing faith is the number of baptisms, the persistence of personal prayers, and the belief in a Creator. Quebec sociologists have, in fact, noted each of these trends.[64] Though they may be understood as societal vestiges shorn of religious meaning, caretakers view them as reflective of a deep underlying Catholic faith, made manifest in how their friends, neighbors, and children interact with the wayside crosses. Jean-Marc Thouin, in Saint-Jovite, says, "People need to connect to something that's important to them." He continues: "I've seen a lot of people who aren't practicing stop in front of the cross and kneel and confess/confide [*se confier*]. . . . They need a sign and it's a sign. . . . They were in a state like, depressed, and they stop to pray, confess. They even confide in me [if I am working on the cross]. [They say] I have sins or they make the sign of the cross. Sometimes people don't want to go into churches but they'll take a walk in nature and stop by the cross and say an interior prayer. I pray for them and with them too."

Caretakers make sense of the non-practicing majority in ambivalent, even contradictory ways. Few caretakers feel that walking in nature, for example, suffices on its own. Almost 90 percent of them do, in fact, participate in Mass and confession, though they simultaneously downplay their value for others. Partly, their perspective reflects a pragmatism borne of necessity. Priests divide their time between far-flung parishes, and most rural caretakers have far less regular access to sacraments, which necessarily lessens their importance in terms of everyday or weekly practice. Priests also constitute a particular sticking point for the caretakers' non-practicing family and friends, who often associate them with sex scandals and misogyny. Caretakers respond that this inordinate focus on clergy altogether misses the heart of contemporary Catholicism, which resides in laypeople themselves.[65] The non-practicing majority—with its sincere, interiorized belief—is actually, they extrapolate, in harmony with current

Catholic theology, though, as Pierette notes above, most do not even realize it. Wayside crosses thus provide a crucial sign for non-practicing Quebecers, a material reminder that triggers sincere but latent belief, that may even impel passersby to fall to their knees, pray, and confess. They may not need a priest, say caretakers, but they still need God.

## The Aesthetics of Contemporary Devotion

Catholic devotionalism is material and sensory: candles, flowers and incense, kneeling, kissing, and touching.[66] As historians point out, significant aesthetic changes accompanied theological ones in midcentury North American Catholicism. Church interiors were revamped to promote unmediated lay contact with the divine and to express the newly participatory Mass with its Eucharistic focus: reredos and communion railings were torn down, side altars and the saints in them removed. Catholic intellectuals promoted modern art over representational devotional cards and statues. The uncluttered, unadorned church, once so representative of Protestantism, became a Catholic ideal too—though recently a backlash in some parishes has "erased the hard edges of Vatican II modernism" by restoring devotional materials like the crucifix.[67]

The debate about aesthetics is heated because it inevitably also concerns "ways of imagining, encountering, and experiencing the sacred," a conversation that in North America is often deeply classist and gendered.[68] Indeed, elite promoters of Quebec's wayside crosses early on tried to discourage aesthetics they felt were incompatible with their vision of a humble, pious rural people. Arthur Saint-Pierre, the leader of Montreal's Société Saint-Jean-Baptiste, introduced the society's 1915 *croix de chemin* story contest, and subsequent book, with, "From the cross [that is] completely simple, completely unified, to the cross, happily rare, that is overcrowded with colors and ornaments where piety is expressed with more naïve sincerity than good taste."[69] Half a century later, when Quebec scholars took up the crosses' cause, their aesthetic preferences were reversed. No longer interested in promoting a certain kind of Catholicism, they valued those crosses that were *most* ornamented. The intricate, colorful wood carvings had become folk art.[70]

Today, all caretakers agree that a cross must be beautiful, though they are divided as to whether beauty resides in simplicity or ornamentation. Caretakers who build unadorned white crosses (or reconstruct older ornamental crosses as simple ones) claim that their beauty resides in their meaning. Representative of this view is the seventy-three-year-old Henri-Paul

Gagné, who built a new cross in 1993. Although fond memories of the wayside cross near his childhood home inspired him—and, as a tribute, he planted the same flowers at the new cross's base—he chose not to recreate its ornate decorations: "I put up a plain white one because, regardless of religion, the Catholic religion or the Protestants, they believe in Christ too. So this cross serves *all* religions. When they pass there they can pray at it, because there're no thingamajigs [*gugusses*]. The priest said it's a cross of *peace*. It really makes for something beautiful." The emphasis on peace is important, given the troublesome history of Protestantism in Quebec, which French Canadian Catholics associate with *anglo-saxonisme* and thus with the enemy and oppressor. The simple wayside cross expresses a major reversal: a new openness toward Protestants and the recognition that practicing Christians in Quebec have more in common than not. For caretakers, it is the hallmark of a modern Quebec and of a post–Vatican II Catholicism.

Those who consider an ornamented cross more beautiful do so because it faithfully represents the past (if it is an exact replica of an earlier cross) and because it arrests attention. Passersby stop to photograph ornate crosses more often, they note. All caretakers agree, however, on one major point: a cross is most beautiful when it is clearly being cared for. Marielle Lemay says, "We built [our cross] in metal so it will be beautiful for five hundred years! A cross in wood that's not maintained isn't beautiful. I told myself, that in X years, people will still stop and it will always be beautiful." Caretakers thus conceive of beauty differently than do the scholars and heritage professionals who focus on the oldest and most traditional crosses. For caretakers, an iron replacement is easier to maintain and, on that ground alone, may be more beautiful than its wooden predecessor. As result, whereas 90 percent of crosses were wooden in the 1970s, many are made of metal today (p. 110).[71]

Flowers and landscaping—of little interest to heritage experts—constitute another major component of a cross's beauty, tied to the aesthetics of newness and care (pp. 108 and 109). As living things, they attest to regular upkeep. Without it, grass grows too long, flowers droop, and shrubs grow wild. Although *croix de chemin* are associated with nature and rural areas, for caretakers it is crucial that they not be mistaken for natural topographic features. Colorful flowers, a big red heart, or a brilliant white frame all draw the gaze and confirm the intentional nature of this human construction. Otherwise, a cross might fade into the everyday scenery on an oft-traveled road; the cross then ceases to function as a powerful spiritual *point de repère* (point of reference), as caretakers often say, that jogs Catholics' memory and turns their thoughts to God.

The crosses materialize caretakers' private faith and send it out into the world. Raymonde Proulx, a sixty-two-year-old in the village of Sainte-Gertrude-Manneville, puts it succinctly: "When the *croix de chemin* are beautifully maintained, it says, *yes*, there are still people who confess the Catholic religion." It is, she notes, a symbol of Quebec history and of Christianity in general but, most of all, it is "a sign of vitality"—proof that a living faith animates its caretakers. "The cross," she concludes, "is a concrete example of being in harmony with your values."

## Remapping Wayside Cross Devotions

Scholars predicted the demise of Quebec's wayside crosses, and popular media has portrayed them as a forgotten remnant of the past—though they are still being built and restored in rural regions throughout the province. When observers note this trend, they generally explain it in one of two ways: as a sign of Quebecers' respect for their heritage—an answer that elides or denies religious motives—or, conversely, as a sign of rural people's retrograde Catholicism, which defies (urban) Quebec's inevitable progress toward a secular modernity. Clearly, neither explanation suffices. Caretakers view heritage as inseparable from the living faith they nurture. Wayside crosses are thus undeniably religious objects. Yet caretakers are by no means traditionalists. The crosses retain value precisely because of their repositioning as compatible with, even representative of, contemporary Catholicism and modern Quebec society.

This conclusion speaks more broadly to how, as studies of the Second Vatican Council's societal impact move beyond older paradigms of rupture and continuity, it opens up room to also reevaluate assumptions about Catholic devotionalism. Wayside crosses were never the static entity often portrayed, flourishing before Vatican II and then plummeting into irreversible decline. A more helpful approach views devotions as in flux and changing, without minimizing the transitions that have occurred. For cross caretakers, these transitions include new theologies of lay participation, as well as government projects to widen roads or centralize the education system. To see how Vatican II has been lived, we need thick descriptions that take all these factors into account. The result is that caretakers still pray at their crosses and maintain them, though they have come to view such acts differently from their parents. They rarely focus on communal devotions and never pray for protection against agricultural plagues and fires. Instead, they emphasize that their devotional labor is extraliturgical and voluntary, in consonance with contemporary

Catholicism's recognition of laypeople's personal responsibility for their faith. They have repositioned the wayside cross as fundamentally about an individual's relationship with God.

Caretakers understand contemporary Catholicism in often ambivalent, even contradictory ways. Though they attend Mass regularly, they insist that institutional Catholicism is not fundamental to being a Catholic. It is a paradox familiar to western Catholics everywhere as people have come to self-define as "believing but not practicing" (and the variant, "spiritual but not religious"). Scholars and Church officials note that this view is particularly pronounced in Quebec, where religion and French Canadian identity have been so closely intertwined. Ironically, then, caretakers have come to see the construction of very large and very public signs of Christianity as compatible with provincial modernization and secularization. For them, today's crosses are for everyone—part of the nationalist ideal of a shared civic heritage and, at the same time, a reminder for the believing-not-practicing majority who need (and subconsciously want, caretakers add) signs that impel them to think of God. Wayside crosses signal a relationship with Jesus, with the Catholic Church, and with the "ancestors," while simultaneously evoking a distinct Quebec heritage. By embracing all these potential meanings, caretakers position this devotional practice as a powerful, evolving sign of faith.

NOTES

All translations from French are my own. Thank you to Jean Simard for helpful clarifications and to David A. Morgan for valuable comments on an earlier draft. I am also indebted to my hardworking research assistants, Eleni Psarudis, Camille Perrault, Daniel Saenz, and Josée Roy.

1. For example, Bélanger, "À la croisée des chemins."

2. Simard, *Le Québec pour terrain*, 61–72; Joly, "Des croix de chemin en quête de protecteurs," 41–67; Carpentier, *Les croix de chemin*, 31, 54–55.

3. Simard, *Le Québec pour terrain*, 5; Simard, Milot, and Bouchard, *Un patrimoine méprisé*. Simard's first article on the crosses, in 1972, was titled, "Witnesses to the Passing of Faith" ("Témoins d'un passé de foi. Perspectives," *La Presse*, June 17, 1972, 20–22).

4. Ouellet, *Les croix de chemin dans la MRC les Basques*, 35. These themes date back a century. See, for example, Roy, "Préface," 13; Farly, "La croix du p'tit rocher," 114.

5. These three descriptors are the subheadings in Christiano, "The Trajectory of Catholicism in Twentieth-Century Quebec." This narrative is ubiquitous in popular media. For example, see recently on Radio-Canada, Maheu, "L'histoire oubliée des croix de chemin."

6. As I point out below, Jean Simard—still the expert on Quebec's crosses—has since noted that his predictions were in error.

7. I include new crosses and reconstructions. The number is an estimate based on eight books detailing the crosses in particular parishes, and on a 2012–13 telephone survey conducted by my research assistants of 398 parishes, 199 of which had crosses. It is an estimate because we were not able to reach every parish (another 400 parishes were called without success) nor could all parish assistants and priests provide accurate counts.

8. From the parish survey, my research assistants identified fifty follow-ups representing four major trends: crosses that were (a) privately owned, (b) on public land, (c) restored by the Chevaliers de Colomb, or (d) used in municipal events. Long-form interviews of one to two hours were conducted by phone (by my research assistants and me) or in person (by me). On three occasions, I spent two to three days visiting caretakers in their villages. I also conducted twelve interviews with local historical societies and Chevaliers de Colomb leaders.

9. Parent, "Dieu, le capitalisme et le développement local," 134.

10. Kane, "American Catholic Studies at a Crossroads," 267. A three-year project, *Lived History of Vatican II*, is underway at the Cushwa Center and includes the work of Gilles Routhier on Quebec.

11. Meunier, Laniel, and Demers, "Permanence et recomposition de la 'religion culturelle,'" 95, 106–7, 122. Note that rates are higher outside of Montreal (e.g., 97.3 percent are baptized in the Diocese of Quebec).

12. O'Toole, *Habits of Devotion*, 3–4; Baggett, *Sense of the Faithful*, 22–23.

13. Lucier, "La révolution tranquille," 19–20; Bélanger, "The Three Pillars of Survival."

14. Morisset, "Une île, un zoo, une ville," 153–54.

15. Roy, "Préface," 14.

16. Massicotte, "Avant-Propos," 22. On tourism, see Morisset, "Une île, un zoo, une ville," 152,156–57.

17. "Les croix de chemin à travers la patrie canadienne," in Joly, "Des croix de chemin," 46.

18. Roy, "Préface," 14.

19. This myth is beyond my scope and covered elsewhere. I concur here with Simard, *Le Québec pour le terrain*, 73.

20. Ibid., 300, 302–7; Timmermann, "Highways to Heaven (and Hell)," 391–92.

21. Martin, "La fonction polyvalente des croix à la fin du Moyen-Âge," 299.

22. Admittedly, my comparison juxtaposes fourteenth- to seventeenth-century Europe with modern Quebec. More research on modern Europe is needed to clarify these differences.

23. Simard and Milot, *Les croix de chemin du Québec*, 1–4; Timmermann, "Highways to Heaven (and Hell)," 393.

24. Survey in Carpentier, *Les croix de chemin*, 103, 112–13; Frisk, "May, Mary's Month."

25. Schiller, *Iconography of Christian Art*, 184–85.

26. Ibid., 187. I do not include Quebec calvaries. See note 70 below.

27. Karel, "Alexandre Carli," 146.

28. About 40 percent of crosses had a niche in the 1970s, 55 percent of which contained Mary. Carpentier, *Les croix de chemin*, 373–76. Timmerman, "Highways to Heaven (and Hell)," 391, also notes that the stylistic features of European crosses bore no relation to the reason for construction.

29. Simard, personal communication, May 15, 2013.

30. Bélanger, "The Quiet Revolution."

31. Meunier, Laniel, and Demers, "Permanence et recomposition," 107. On religion in villages, see Parent, "Pratique religieuse et espaces-temps sociaux dans un village québécois," 182.

32. Carpentier, *Les croix de chemin*, 103. Saint-Pierre, "Introduction," 16; Racine, "École québécoise, modernité et religion," 277–91.

33. Joly, "Des croix de chemin,"42.

34. Genest, "Avant-Propos," viii; Simard, interview with the author, October 11, 2012; Joly, interview with the author, October 10, 2012.

35. Simard's 1994 publication of the "top" 704 crosses was meant to encourage local restorations. Simard and Milot, *Les croix de chemin du Québec*, 1, 14. See also Carpentier, *Les croix de chemin*, 391.

36. Télé-Quebec is a provincial station. The university chairs are at Université de Québec à Montréal, Université Laval (Québec), and Université de Montréal.

37. Turgeon and Saint-Pierre, "Building an Integrated Multimedia Digital Database," 414–15; Simard, personal interview, October 11, 2012; Conseil du Patrimoine Religieux du Québec, "2012–2013 Budget Appropriation for Québec Religious Heritage Restoration"; Conseil du Patrimoine Religieux du Québec, "Restauration du patrimoine religieux."

38. Turgeon and Saint-Pierre, "Building an Integrated Multimedia Digital Database," 411, 414; Joly, "Des croix de chemin," 43–44; Lefebvre, "Introduction," 23.

39. Gauthier, "Autour du livre *Les églises du Québec*," 203–8. On communal heritage, for example, see Groulx (the director of Quebec's Religious Heritage Council), "Préface," 17–18.

40. See Joly, "Des croix de chemin," 43.

41. Local journalists are also more likely to cover their activities in the *hebdomadaires* (weekly newspapers). Of the thirty-six articles on the crosses published from 2006 to 2012 and available in a publicly accessible database, sixteen feature work by historical societies, five by municipal councils, and three by parishes (twelve were "other"). Only two articles mentioned that caretakers believe in God.

42. Adapted from Gauthier, St-André, and Roy, *Nos croix de chemin*, 5.

43. In the 1970s, 13.8 percent of crosses commemorated events (though note that 62 percent of crosses had unknown origins). Carpentier, *Les croix de chemin*, 42.

44. Drolet, *L'Ordre des Chevaliers de Colomb*, 175, 183–86, 203–4, 213.

45. Lefebvre, *Christophe Colomb et l'Ordre des Chevaliers de Colomb*, 110–12.

46. Tanguay, general director of the Chevaliers de Colomb, personal interview, May 6, 2013.

47. I surveyed *Le Colombien* from 1968 to 2011, and extant issues from the monthly bulletin (1958–67), as well as *La Revue Colombienne* (1943–46). The crosses are first mentioned in the late 1970s but not featured regularly (or as restoration projects) until the mid-1980s.

48. Thouin, personal interview, March 21, 2013.

49. Dillon and Wink, *In the Course of a Lifetime*, 81–83.

50. Gauthier, St-André, and Roy, *Nos croix de chemin*, 45–47.

51. Massicotte, "Avant-Propos," 22. Crosses today stand longer because the wood is treated.

52. Carpentier, *Les croix de chemin*, 99.

53. Mager and Cantin, "Religion, modernité, Québec," 3. Simard, Milot, and Bouchard, *Un patrimoine méprisé*, passim.

54. Bibby, "La religion à la carte au Québec," 161, 175.

55. Carpentier, *Les croix de chemin*, 9.

56. This is true of about 10 percent of crosses today (and 50 percent of new crosses since the 1980s). See Simard's 1970s surveys in Carpentier, *Les croix de chemin*, 42–68, 70, 79.

57. Saint-Pierre, "Introduction," 16.

58. Courteau, "Scènes d'autrefois et scènes d'aujourd'hui," 107.

59. Germain, personal interview, March 15, 2013; Lemay, personal interview, March 27, 2013.

60. This reflects the disappearance of the novena and the communal rosary more generally. Bursts of renewed interest in month of Mary prayers often accompany (re)constructions, like Marielle Lemay's above. On parallel novena trends in the United States, see Chinnici, "The Catholic Community at Prayer."

61. Caretakers often brought up a much-publicized legal case about Sikh kirpans in school (they confused Sikhs with Muslims), which sparked the lengthy "accommodation crisis" in 2008.

62. Carpentier, *Les croix de chemin*, 42.

63. Rymarz, "Forward Thinking," 1–2.

64. Meunier, Laniel, and Demers, "Permanence et recomposition," 89. In a well-known article ("La religion à la carte au Québec"), the sociologist Reginald Bibby argues that it does indicate continuing Catholicism.

65. Bibby, "La religion à la carte au Québec," 167; Parent, "Pratique religieuse et espaces-temps," 186–87.

66. See, for example, Orsi, "'The Infant of Prague's Nightie,'" 8–9.

67. McDannell, *Material Christianity*, 163–97; Schloeder, *Architecture in Communion*, 16, 23; McDannell, *The Spirit of Vatican II*, 211.

68. Orsi, "'The Infant of Prague's Nightie,'" 3.

69. Saint-Pierre, "Introduction," 15.

70. Simard and Milot, *Les croix de chemin du Québec*, 10–14. I do not include the (comparatively rare) Quebec calvaries. They include Jesus's body, often carved by artists like Louis Jobin, and therefore hold special value for heritage experts and historians. See, for example, Bourget, "Les croix de chemins et les calvaires."

71. Carpentier, *Les croix de chemin*, 197.

# EPILOGUE

*Lucas Van Rompay, Sam Miglarese, and David Morgan*

In the words of John W. O'Malley, the authoritative North American historian of the Council, "Vatican II was unprecedented in the history of councils for the notice it took of changes in society at large and for its refusal to see them in globally negative terms as devolutions from an older and happier era, despite the fact that the council met just shortly after the bloodiest half-century in the history of the human race." Furthermore, the Second Vatican Council "recognized that a profound shift in human awareness was taking place in the substitution of a dynamic and more evolutionary concept of nature for a static one."[1] In addition to their genuine recognition of changing times, the Council Fathers also introduced a new style in which to communicate their newly gained insights. This new style—again in O'Malley's words—was "less autocratic and more collaborative, a style willing to seek out and listen to different viewpoints and to take them into account, a style eager to find common ground with 'the other,' a style open and above board, a style less unilateral in its decision-making, a style committed to fair play and to working with persons and institutions outside the Catholic community."[2]

What O'Malley thus aptly summarizes as the Council's unique features and, one may add, unique strengths, may also be seen as the Council's vulnerability. By opening itself up to its own faithful and to the world at large, the Church hierarchy also brought itself into a potentially uncomfortable situation, exposing itself to conversation partners whose expectations could not be controlled and whose criticism could not always be avoided. Moreover, in spite of relatively low expectations at the beginning of the Council, the conciliar process rapidly gained steam and in an experience of "collective effervescence," broad support emerged for what could be termed progressive positions,[3] in favor of openness, new structures of authority, individual freedom, the role of the laity, and respect for non-Catholic and non-Christian traditions. Some attributed this new dynamism to the workings of the Holy Spirit, others to effective social networking. But the outcome of the Council, as laid down in many of its documents, was more innovative, more visionary, and more forward-looking than most people, both insiders and outsiders, had anticipated. Conservative forces of either traditionalist bishops or the Roman Curia only rarely won the day. This wave of optimism, the enthusiasm about the progressive victory, led to a sober awakening once the Council ended and the opposing views—passionately fought for and partly covered up in carefully balanced theological language—resurfaced in real life, perhaps even more polarized than before. The seeds for a complex reception history and a burdensome legacy were planted.

O'Malley rightly points out that big issues such as the question of continuity versus change, center versus periphery, and firmness versus flexibility—issues that go to the heart of the Catholic Church in our day and directly touch on Catholic identity—"by their very nature . . . do not admit of definitive resolution one way or the other. Their essence is to be in tension." Rather than denying it, the Church must, in his view, "maintain and exploit the dialectic" between the two extremes.[4] This concept of tension provides a helpful tool for contextualizing and assessing the five essays of our volume. We should add, however, that the dialectic or tension between the two opposing perspectives should not be understood as the perpetual motion of a pendulum, swinging one way and the other, always receding and always coming back. Rather, the Church itself is an agent, capable of steering and even controlling the process. The Church will see it as its role to be in conversation with both sides, holding the institution together and maintaining a fruitful interaction within and beyond the traditional boundaries.

Building on O'Malley's insights and fully recognizing the unique and innovative work of the Council, the historian Stephen Schloesser has drawn attention to the Council's larger historical context. The Council Fathers had the tragedy of World War II still fresh in their minds, and they found themselves in the midst of the Cold War, which divided the world into two opposing camps. They saw the threat of nuclear annihilation and were witness to the ongoing process of decolonization and the loss of European hegemony in the world.[5] While these factors had a decisive impact on what "happened" at the Council and created a strong sense of urgency, they leave subsequent generations—divorced from the Council's original context, and selectively remembering and forgetting what it was all about—somewhat uncertain as to how to implement the Council's legacy in their own day. New frames of interpretation need to be found.

In the ideology and self-perception of the Catholic Church, no area has seen, during the Council, more radical change than that of Catholic views of other religions—Judaism in the first place and the other religious traditions as well. Largely in response to the horrors of the Shoah, the Council Fathers questioned and revised earlier Catholic views of Judaism and, in the Declaration on the Relation of the Church to Non-Christian Religions (*Nostra Aetate*), expressed with regard to both Judaism and the other religious traditions a much more positive and respectful attitude, culminating in the view that "all nations are one community" (*Nostra Aetate*, 1). The groundwork for this new attitude is laid out in the two key documents, *Nostra Aetate* and *Dignitatis Humanae*, which declares that every human person must have the right to religious freedom. Leo D. Lefebure points out in his present essay, however, that other documents as well endorsed and illuminated the same broader mentality shift, which following the Council has become the solid foundation of Catholic teaching in the past fifty years. In spite of some vocal opposition, the change has been widely accepted and will be irrevocable. At the same time, however, there have been, on the part of the Church authorities, some notable relapses into pre–Vatican II thinking—unfortunate statements or glitches, provoked or unprovoked. These raise questions about the overall profundity of the change and leave the faithful and the non-Christian conversation partners wondering where the Catholic Church stands in the process of translating and implementing the high ideals of the Council with regard to non-Christian religions. It is only in recent months, following the election of Pope Francis, that a more positive atmosphere has made itself felt in the statements and actions of the Church.[6] Here, as in other areas, the appearance of Pope Francis reminds us that, in spite of the highly textualized nature of Catholicism, real change is not only wrought through texts but must take place in the hearts and minds of people.

In a number of areas the Council Fathers acted in response to major changes in society at large, thereby attempting to synchronize developments in the Church with those in society and to redefine the Church's position in the modern world. This need for *aggiornamento*, for a bringing up to date, in fact constituted one of the major driving forces behind the Council. But many of the changes in the world in the late 1950s and 1960s had their own origins and their own dynamics, and they went their own way, often unaffected or only indirectly affected by the Council decisions. Leslie Woodcock Tentler analyzes the transformation of the American Catholic landscape in the mid-twentieth century, when upward mobility and suburbanization contributed to the final collapse of the American Catholic subculture. In this process of change, the more educated among American Catholics eagerly embraced some of the Council reforms. To some extent, however, these reforms had a centrifugal effect. In debates over the use of birth control, divorce and remarriage, and liturgical innovation, laypeople often ended up taking things into their own hands, and the clergy had little choice but to follow along. In her discussion of race relations in the industrial city of Detroit, Tentler shows how the Council had two mutually opposing effects. On the one hand, it inspired Bishop Dearden's efforts for reconciliation between the races in downtown Detroit, while on the other hand, with its emphasis on the role of laypeople, it gave Dearden's lay opponents ammunition to resist their bishop's authority. Tentler's essay gives us the lay perspective in our study of the Council's reception, as well as the specific American context, focusing on the years immediately following the Council. In interesting ways, the history of the Council and its aftermath here intersects with an important chapter of American social history.

Both for the inner workings of the Church and for the Church operating in the world, the exercise of authority is a central issue. In this respect, the Council introduced important changes, redefining authority as service and, in Catherine E. Clifford's words, marking "a definitive shift away from a pyramidal, monarchical conception of the Church." Authority evokes the question of collegiality, and since the First Vatican Council had so exalted the authority of the pope (who in the exercise of his office concerning faith and morals was officially declared infallible), many thought that the Second Vatican Council should somewhat redress the imbalance by positively redefining the role of the bishops. This is indeed what happened in the Constitution on the Church (*Lumen Gentium*). Clifford's essay chronicles the origin of this constitution and much of the discussion surrounding it—including stiff opposition from a minority group and direct papal intervention. Even though the text eventually was able to garner overwhelming support, she argues that the problematic process surrounding it negatively affected its subsequent reception within the Church. Fifty years later the Church still does not have a system in place that fully honors episcopal collegiality.

As for the lay participation in the exercise of authority, the Council recognized the "priestly, prophetic, and royal office" of the people of God (Decree on the Apostolate of the Laity, *Apostolicam Actuositatem*, 2), that is, of all the baptized faithful, and thus opened the path for giving them a more significant role to play at the center of the Church.[7] But here again, the postconciliar follow-up has proven minimal at best. It is difficult to escape the impression that the pendulum has been deliberately held back in one corner. Catholics had to wait for the charismatic figure of

Pope Francis to infuse new energy into the Roman structures of authority. By convening, in the fall of 2014, an Extraordinary General Assembly of the Synod of Bishops—an institution whose 1965 origin and subsequent development Clifford briefly traces in her essay—the pontiff courageously initiated a new conversation on a number of difficult questions surrounding "the family." Reactions to the first session of the synod have been mixed and only the follow-up sessions in 2015 and beyond will tell how this new experience of dialogue will affect the patterns of decision making and authority within the Catholic Church.

The Council and the variegated history of its reception have served for the Catholic Church as a learning experience about the limitations of its role and place in the modern world. Better educated than ever before, Catholic laypeople in the late twentieth century had learned to live in a secularized world, in a world in which the non-Christian and the non-Catholic were no longer necessarily seen as the distinct other. They felt empowered to decide for themselves which role they would allow the traditional Church to play in their lives. Not that the Council held no authority in their eyes; but rather than receiving and accepting what the Council Fathers had in store for them, laypeople felt free to select and negotiate the outcome that fitted them best. While it is true that throughout the second half of the twentieth century many left the Church—for reasons partly related and partly unrelated to the Council—others felt committed to stay. But they forged with the Church a new relationship that allowed them to satisfy their own religious needs and to develop their religious life on their own terms. This process may be observed in a number of situations. In many cases it unfolded quietly, with give-and-take on both sides; in other cases it spurred controversy.

A noticeable example of the latter category is discussed in Jill Peterfeso's essay. It was not during the Council or in response to the Council that Catholic women for the first time found their voice or raised their concerns—one should rather consider the larger contexts of feminism and the civil rights movement, which both had only tenuous connections to the Catholic Church. But the overwhelmingly male event of the Council, with hardly any female participation, and the deliberate decision that some of the issues most relevant to women—priestly celibacy and women's access to the priesthood—were to be banned from the conciliar discussions did not fail to disappoint, frustrate, or alienate large groups of Catholic women. How could a Council, hailed for its openness and progressive vision, not take note of the fact that half of the Church's active members were female?

Catholic women responded in different ways to the fact that some of the issues of importance to them had not been considered and that for others the Council Fathers presented an exclusively male perspective. While the Decree on the Ministry and the Life of Priests (*Presbyterorum Ordinis*) includes women in the priesthood of the faithful as far as the mission of the Church is concerned, the rejection of women's eligibility to ordination is based on the statement, in the same decree, that "priests are signed with a special character and are conformed (*configurantur*) to Christ the Priest in such a way that they can act in the person of Christ the Head" (2). This means that—in the view of the Council Fathers—the efficacious grace of the sacrament of orders empowers the priest to act *in persona Christi*, to undertake Christ's headship, his pastoral role in the Church. Yet by the mid-1970s this had come also to mean that women, in contrast to men, did not reflect the image or the *persona* of Christ's maleness.

In response to the Council women started arguing for more gender equality in the Church. As for the question of women's access to the priesthood, the women studied by Peterfeso do not speak out against the Council. Rather, they insert themselves into the logic of the Council, thus claiming the Council for themselves and reading it through their own interpretative lenses. They do so by pointing to Council documents, in particular the Constitutions on the Church (*Lumen Gentium*) and on the Church in the Modern World (*Gaudium et Spes*), which emphasize lay participation and condemn all kinds of discrimination. Their frustration with exclusion from the conciliar and postconciliar processes emboldens them to claim for themselves the spirit of the Council. As a matter of fact, the Catholic Church, by opening itself to the world, lost the exclusive control of its institutions, of its documents and their interpretation, and of its values. These they henceforth had to share with others. The question as to whether the womenpriests are within the Church (as the women maintain) or outside the Church (as the authorities assert by excommunicating them) loses much of its relevance in view of the larger issue at stake, the question of the legitimate interpretation of conciliar documents. The Council has become a two-edged sword.

Peterfeso's essay, therefore, pointedly again raises the question of interpretation. By using Council texts in support of their case, the womenpriests not only engage in the selective reading (and selective ignoring) of specific passages—while imposing on these passages their own interpretational hierarchy—but they also dissociate the texts from their authors and from (explicit or implicit) authorial intent. What does this mean for the nature of the texts? As the product of consultation and compromise, texts once created have a life of their own, and whatever they have to offer—including their complexities, inherent tensions, and contradictions—no longer lies exclusively in the hands of the ones who created them or of the institution that issued them. Rather, they become the common property of later readers and recipients. Council texts, therefore, are woven into the fabric of lived religion and lend themselves to being used as a frame of reference or a source of inspiration in all discussions at the heart of the Church.

Hillary Kaell's essay presents a different case of empowered laypeople and the creation of new meaning in the postconciliar age. The wayside crosses of Quebec were doomed to disappear or to be reduced to the status of lifeless monuments, as they seemed out of touch with conciliar guidelines on liturgical reform. Laypeople succeeded, however, in instilling new life in them. Through a complex process of selective (re)interpretation and (re)negotiation of key concepts of the Council—such as lay participation, openness to the world, and a positive attitude toward non-Catholics and non-Christians—they made the crosses into a new, revitalized expression of their postconciliar religiosity and their own Catholic identity, with little interference from the Church authorities. The process of revitalization has proved a fascinating combination of scholarly authority in the efforts of the ethnologist Jean Simard, government support through the Council for Religious Heritage, and the Catholic laity of Quebec, many of whom do not wish to see their religious and national culture vanish. In one sense the preservation of the crosses has curbed the impact of the Vatican Council on the deaccentuation of traditional devotionalism by celebrating the crosses as artifacts of the faith. At the same time, however, the crosses have been transformed into specimens of cultural heritage, objects of value not only to Catholics but to all Quebecers. It manifests a cultural survival, but also a subtle change in register.

Additionally, the shift since the 1980s to more durable media also helped ensure the crosses' survival. The older devotional forms were crafted from wood; recent iterations are fabricated from metal and coated with industrial-grade paint. The material culture of traditional devotional life did not eschew the use of finite materials since these proved more affordable and readily available, but also because they were replaceable over time. Icons were refreshed, broken statues repaired or replaced, paintings cleaned and retouched. The new steel crosses dotting the Quebec landscape were made with the intention of lasting. They remember their antecedents, as Kaell points out, but they do so within the matrix of modern, industrial durability. The difference makes sense, since the latest generation of crosses, with their new religious messages, was fabricated within the framework of a new public language: the discourse of cultural heritage that Kaell productively explores.

Vatican II may be read in many ways, but one important way fixes attention on an ongoing tension in the Catholic tradition. This tension is located between a centralized hierarchy of authority invested in the Roman Curia and its *pontifex maximus*, the bishop of Rome, and the vast field of lay piety set in everyday life. The two have always comprised the particular character of Roman Catholicism. They may clash in different ways. For example, John Paul II did not feel moved to support the efforts among liberation theologians in Latin America since he strongly opposed Marxist thought and social experimentation, even though Catholic theologians in Latin America presented a case of endorsing Catholicism at the grass roots and foregrounded social and economic justice as the primary aims of Jesus of Nazareth. On the other hand, John XXIII initiated a Council dedicated to reform within the tradition that led to diminishing the degree of lay investment in certain saints' devotions and liturgical traditions. The wake of the Council has seen a counterreaction among some Catholics, who want to revive traditional forms of practice and worship. In each case, a hierarchy that claims to interpret Church tradition collides with lay practice and grassroots initiatives that represent Catholicism as lived religion. Whether progressive or conservative, recognizing the pressure of lived religion is important, since it presses against the edifice of authority, sometimes with dramatic results. The movement to compel the hierarchy to deal more forcefully with priests accused of sexual abuse represents a significant example. In other instances, the hierarchy is not moved at all. Think of the large following that supported the recognition of the apparition of Our Lady of Medjugorje (Bosnia and Herzegovina) as authentic, which did nothing to persuade the Vatican to approve it. Change happens slowly within the Catholic Church, largely because of its built-in conservative tendency owing to dogma as a living tradition. Protestantism possesses a different sociology of change since its sectarian nature facilitates transformation, or at least throws much less resistance in its path.

Among the essays of this volume, three—those by Tentler, Peterfeso, and Kaell—focus on lay responses to the Council. In the three essays one comes across various segments of the Catholic lay population that have found their distinct ways of negotiating what they saw as the key values of the Council. Lefebure's and Clifford's essays, while paying more attention to the institutional perspective, keep the focus on laypeople and on the broader world as well. Exploring the impact of the Council on subsequent generations, therefore, is an exercise in studying the processes by which the "sea changes" of the Council are absorbed within new interpretational frames and in different contexts.[8] These processes have become even more complicated as all-encompassing narratives and larger stories have lost their attraction in the age of postmodernity—as outlined in the influential report of the French philosopher Jean-François Lyotard, *La condition postmoderne*, commissioned by the government of Quebec in the 1970s.[9] Instead, fragmentation and diversity have come to characterize postmodern discourses of knowledge.

Committed to many of the same causes, but not always bound by common purpose or shared strategy, the Catholic hierarchy and its lay constituencies will continue to discern what the Council's significance for the Church and the world will be. The leadership of Pope Francis—new in content and in tone—seems to offer opportunities for the main protagonists within the Church to reposition themselves and to explore fresh approaches to many of the old problems. His attitude seems to be reflected in the now iconic words "Who am I to judge?"—spoken during an interview on July 29, 2013. At the same time, within the global world of the Catholic Church significant changes have taken place and continue to take place. For reasons both internal and external to the Church, Roman Catholicism is losing strength in many of the countries where it traditionally had a robust presence—Europe, North America, Central and South America—while in other parts of the world it is growing, mainly in Asia and Africa. This changing global landscape will have its effect on the balance of power and on the structures of authority within the Church. While the Second Vatican Council constituted the first truly global council, the global face of Catholicism is very different today from what it was fifty years ago. Will it be possible in this changing world to uphold the legacy of Vatican II and to deal with some of its unfinished business? The long shadow of the Council will have its challenges and surprises.[10]

NOTES

1. O'Malley, *What Happened at Vatican II*, 297.

2. Ibid., 307–8. O'Malley's focus on the question of style as a new hermeneutic key to understanding the Council has proven influential in subsequent studies. See, e.g., Famerée, *Vatican II comme style*, a collection of essays from 2012.

3. Coleman, "Vatican II as a Social Movement."

4. O'Malley, *What Happened at Vatican II*, 12.

5. Schloesser, "Against Forgetting."

6. For some thoughts of the new pope on this topic, see Bergoglio and Skorka, *On Heaven and Earth*.

7. For a broader discussion of the concept of Church authority and its reception, see Gaillardetz, *Teaching with Authority*, especially part 4.

8. This is a phrase frequently used, e.g., in Schloesser, "Against Forgetting."

9. Lyotard, *La condition postmoderne*. The report was first published in 1979.

10. For a more theologically oriented discussion of some of the problems inherent in the reception of the Council, see several contributions to the volume edited by M. Lamberigts and L. Kenis, *Vaticanum II*, with an introductory essay by the editors, "Het tweede Vaticaans Concilie (1962–1965): Een *casus belli*?," 9–30.

# Bibliography

## DOCUMENTS OF THE SECOND VATICAN COUNCIL

Tanner, Norman P., S.J., ed. *Decrees of the Ecumenical Councils*. Vol. 2. Washington, D.C.: Georgetown University Press, 1990.

### The Four Constitutions

On the Sacred Liturgy, *Sacrosanctum Concilium* (SC), 820–43
On the Church, *Lumen Gentium* (LG), 849–900
On Divine Revelation, *Dei Verbum* (DV), 971–81
On the Church in the Modern World, *Gaudium et Spes* (GS), 1069–1135

### The Nine Decrees

On the Mass Media, *Inter Mirifica* (IM), 843–49
On the Catholic Eastern Churches, *Orientalium Ecclesiarium* (OE), 900–907
On Ecumenism, *Unitatis Redintegratio* (UR), 908–20
On Bishops, *Christus Dominus* (CD), 921–39
On the Renewal of Religious Life, *Perfectae Caritatis* (PC), 939–47
On the Training of Priests, *Optatum Totius* (OC), 947–59
On the Apostolate of the Laity, *Apostolicam Actuositatem* (AA), 981–1001
On Missionary Activity, *Ad Gentes* (AG), 1011–42
On the Ministry and the Life of Priests, *Presbyterorum Ordinis* (PO), 1042–69

### The Three Declarations

On Christian Education, *Gravissimum Educationis* (GE), 959–68
On Non-Christian Religions, *Nostra Aetate* (NA), 968–71
On Religious Liberty, *Dignitatis Humanae* (DH), 1001–11

## MANUSCRIPT COLLECTIONS

Baltimore, Md.
    Archives of the Archdiocese of Baltimore
        Lawrence Shehan Papers, uncatalogued at time of use
            N. N. to Cardinal Lawrence Shehan, May 20, 1966
Detroit, Mich.
    Archives of the Archdiocese of Detroit
        Archbishop's Commission on Human Relations, Box 2, Folder 28
            Sister Maria Goretti, SNDdeN, "Report on Project Blecki," August 3, 1966

"Summary of Project Community," no author given but almost certainly
   Glenmary Sister Juliana; undated, but likely August 1966
Archbishop's Commission on Human Relations Collection, Box 6, Folder 12
   John E. Tobin to Dearden, February 17, 1966
Archbishop's Commission on Human Relations Collection, Box 7, Folder 18
   "Sad Catholic Detroiter" to Dearden, June 25, 1963
Dearden Papers, Box 13, Folder "School Closings"
   Ed Rooney, "Some Thoughts on the School Closings," undated, but 1971;
      prepared for the Parish Council of St. Paul's, Grosse Pointe
Dearden Papers, Box 23 [temporary cataloguing], not yet in folder
   "Archbishop's Meeting with Priests," typescript, March 14, 1968
   Archbishop John Dearden, "Talk to Clergy re: Kerner Report," undated
      typescript, but likely March 14, 1968
Worship Department, Box 1, Folder "Gumbleton (Vicar for Parishes)," 1969–1971
   Fr. Patrick Cooney to Bishop Thomas Gumbleton, April 9, 1969
   Fr. Patrick Cooney to Bishop Thomas Gumbleton, March 30, 1970
Worship Department, Box 2, Folder "Sermon Outlines," 1959–1966
   Sermon outline for the 24th Sunday after Pentecost, Nov. 17, 1963
   Fr. William Sherzer to Msgr. Bernard Kearns, March 5, 1962
Notre Dame, Ind.
   Archives of the University of Notre Dame
      Thomas Gumbleton Papers [CGUM], Box 48, Folder 9
         Fr. Thomas Hinsberg to Dearden, Nov. 27, 1970
      Thomas Gumbleton Papers [CGUM], Box 48, Folder 11
         Anonymous to Dearden, undated, but late 1970 or early 1971

PUBLISHED MATERIALS

"A Common Word." A Common Word Online, http://www.acommonword.com/index
   .php? lang=en&page=option1. June 12, 2013.
Abbott, Walter M., ed. *The Documents of Vatican II*. New York: America Press, 1966.
Abe, Masao. "On John Paul II's View of Buddhism." In *John Paul II and Interreligious
   Dialogue*, edited by Byron L. Sherwin and Harold Kasimow, 108–12. Maryknoll,
   N.Y.: Orbis Books, 1999.
*Acta Synodalia Sacrosancti Concilii Oecumenici Vaticani II*. Vatican City: Typis
   polyglottis Vaticanis, 1970–99.
Aitken, Robert. "The Intrareligious Realization: Ruminations of an American
   Zen Buddhist." In *John Paul II and Interreligious Dialogue*, edited by Byron L.
   Sherwin and Harold Kasimow, 96–107. Maryknoll, N.Y.: Orbis Books, 1999.
Alberigo, Giuseppe, and Joseph A. Komonchak, eds. *History of Vatican II*. Maryknoll,
   N.Y.: Orbis Books, 1996–2006.
"Alexandre Carli." In *Dictionnaire des artistes de langue française en Amérique du
   Nord*, edited by David Karel, 146. Quebec City: Presses de l'Université Laval, 1992.
Alexander, Paul Julius. *The Byzantine Apocalyptic Tradition*. Berkeley: University of
   California Press, 1985.

Allen, John L. "Ordinations Ignite Debate over Tactics: Women Face Excommunication for Actions." *National Catholic Reporter,* July 19, 2002.

———. "Real War on Religion and a Ticking Vatican PR Bomb." *National Catholic Reporter Online,* http://ncronline.org/blogs/all-things-catholic/real-war-religion-and-ticking-vatican-pr-bomb. June 12, 2013.

———. "Seven Women 'Ordained' Priests June 29." *National Catholic Reporter,* July 1, 2002.

Anglican-Roman Catholic International Commission (ARCIC). "Authority in the Church I and II." In *The Final Report.* London: SPCK, 1982.

———. *The Gift of Authority: Authority in the Church III.* Toronto: Anglican Book Centre, 1999.

Association of Roman Catholic Women Priests. "About Us." Association of Roman Catholic Women Priests, www.arcwp.org/about.html. June 22, 2013.

Baggett, Jerome P. *Sense of the Faithful: How American Catholics Live Their Faith.* New York: Oxford University Press, 2009.

Banki, Judith H., and John T. Pawlikowski, eds. *Ethics in the Shadow of the Holocaust.* Franklin, Wisc.: Sheed and Ward, 2001.

Bauman, Chad M. "Identity, Conversion, and Violence: Dalits, Adivasis, and the 2007–08 Riots in Orissa." In *Margins of Faith: Dalit and Tribal Christianity in India,* edited by Rowena Robinson and Joseph Marianus Kujur, 263–90. Thousand Oaks, Calif.: Sage Publications, 2010.

Baverstock, Alasdair. "Pope Francis' Run-In with Benedict XVI over the Prophet Mohammed." *Telegraph,* March 15, 2013, http://www.telegraph.co.uk/news/religion/the-pope/9931030/Pope-Francis-run-in-with-Benedict-XVI-over-the-Prophet-Mohammed.html. March 25, 2014.

Bayly, Michael J. "'We Are All the Rock': An Interview with Roman Catholic Womanpriest Judith McKloskey." *Progressive Catholic Voice,* August 2008, http://www.progressivecatholicvoice.org/enewsletters/index_Aug08.html#Rock. June 22, 2013.

Bea, Augustin Cardinal. *The Church and the Jewish People: A Commentary on the Second Vatican Council's Declaration on the Relation of the Church to Non-Christian Religions.* Translated by Philip Loretz. New York: Harper and Row, 1966.

———. *The Unity of Christians.* New York: Herder and Herder, 1963.

Bélanger, Claude. "The Quiet Revolution." Marianopolis College Online, http://faculty.marianopolis.edu/c.belanger/quebechistory/events/quiet.htm. February 25, 2013.

———. The Three Pillars of Survival." Marianopolis College Online, http://faculty.marianopolis.edu/c.belanger/quebechistory/events/pillars.htm. February 25, 2013.

Bélanger, Mathieu. "À la croisée des chemins." *La Presse,* July 28, 2012, http://www.lapresse.ca/le-droit/dossiers/patrimoine-religieux/201207/27/01-4560068-a-la-croisee-des-chemins.php. March 2, 2013.

Bergoglio, Jorge Mario, and Abraham Skorka, *On Heaven and Earth: Pope Francis on Faith, Family, and the Church in the Twenty-First Century.* New York: Image, 2013.

Bernstein, Carl, and Marco Politi. *His Holiness: John Paul II and the History of Our Time.* New York: Doubleday, 1996.

Bibby, Reginald W. "La religion à la carte au Québec: Un problème d'offre, de demande, ou des deux?" *Globe: Revue internationale d'études québécoises* 11.1 (2008): 151–79.

Bonavoglia, Angela. *Good Catholic Girls: How Women Are Leading the Fight to Change the Church.* New York: HarperCollins, 2005.

Borelli, John, ed. *A Common Word and the Future of Christian-Muslim Relations.* Washington, D.C.: Prince Alwaleed Bin Talal Center for Muslim-Christian Understanding, 2009.

Botte, Bernard. "La collégialité dans le Nouveau Testament et chez les Pères apostoliques." In *Le concile et les conciles: Contribution à la vie conciliaire de l'Église,* edited by Bernard Botte et al., 1–18. Paris: Cerf, 1960.

Bourget, Charles. "Les croix de chemins et les calvaires." Conseil du patrimoine religieux du Québec, http://www.patrimoine religieux.qc.ca/fr/publications/documents/articles.php. March 2, 2013.

Briggs, Kenneth A. *Double Crossed: Uncovering the Catholic Church's Betrayal of American Nuns.* New York: Doubleday, 2006.

Brown, Raymond, Karl P. Donfried, and John Reumann, eds. *Peter in the New Testament: A Collaborative Assessment by Protestant and Roman Catholic Scholars.* Minneapolis: Augsburg Pub. House, 1973.

Burke, Raymond L., and Henry J. Breier. "Declaration of Excommunication of Patricia Fresen, Rose Hudson, and Elsie McGrath." *St. Louis Review,* March 14, 2008, 10.

Cabezón, José Ignacio. "A Buddhist Response to John Paul II." In *John Paul II and Interreligious Dialogue,* edited by Byron L. Sherwin and Harold Kasimow, 113–22. Maryknoll, N.Y.: Orbis Books, 1999.

Call to Action. "Vatican II: Church Forward," http://cta-usa.org/Vatican2/. June 22, 2013.

The Canon Law Society of America. *The Code of Canon Law: A Text and Commentary,* edited by James A. Coriden, Thomas J. Green, and Donald E. Heintschel. New York: Paulist Press, 1985.

Cassidy, Edward Idris Cardinal. *Ecumenism and Interreligious Dialogue: Unitatis Redintegratio, Nostra Aetate.* Mahwah, N.J.: Paulist Press, 2005.

———. "We Remember: A Reflection on the Shoah." Vatican Online. http://www.vatican.va/roman_curia/pontifical_councils/chrstuni/documents/rc_pc_chrstuni_doc_16031998_shoah_en.html. June 11, 2013.

Carpentier, Paul. *Les croix de chemin: Au-delà du signe.* Ottawa: National Museums of Canada, 1981.

Catholic Church. *Catechism of the Catholic Church.* Liguori, Mo.: Liguori Publications, 1994.

———. *English—Latin Sacramentary for the USA.* New York: Catholic Book Publishing Company, 1966.

Celeste, Dagmar Braun. "Soli Deo Amor: Story of a Vagabond Troubadour." In *Women Find a Way: The Movement and Stories of Roman Catholic Womenpriests,* edited by Elsie Hainz McGrath, Bridget Mary Meehan, and Ida Raming, 4–8. College Station, Tex.: Virtualbookworm.com Publishing, 2008.

Cernera, Anthony J. "The Center for Christian-Jewish Understanding of Sacred Heart University: An Example of Fostering Dialogue and Understanding." In *Examining Nostra Aetate after Forty Years: Catholic-Jewish Relations in Our Time,* edited by Anthony J. Cernera, 143–59. Fairfield, Conn.: Sacred Heart University Press, 2007.

Chacour, Elias, and Mary E. Jensen. *We Belong to the Land: The Story of a Palestinian Israeli Who Lives for Peace and Reconciliation*. San Francisco: Harper, 1992.

Chacour, Elias, and Alain Michel. *Faith beyond Despair: Building Hope in the Holy Land*. Translated and edited by Anthony Harvey. London: Canterbury Press Norwich, 2008.

Chadwick, Owen. *A History of the Popes, 1830-1914*. Oxford: Oxford University Press, 2003.

Chatterji, Angana P. *Violent Gods: Hindu Nationalism in India's Present: Narratives from Orissa*. Gurgaon, India: Three Essays Collective, 2009.

Chinnici, Joseph P. "The Catholic Community at Prayer, 1926-1976." In *Habits of Devotion: Catholic Religious Practice in Twentieth-Century America*, edited by James M. O'Toole, 9–88. Ithaca, N.Y.: Cornell University Press, 2004.

"Christian-Buddhist Tensions Turn Violent in Sri Lanka." UCalif.NEWS Online. December 17, 2012, http://www.ucanews.com/news/christian-buddhist-tensions-turn-violent-in-sri-lanka/66874.

Christiano, Kevin J. "The Trajectory of Catholicism in Twentieth-Century Quebec." In *The Church Confronts Modernity: Catholicism in the United States, Ireland and Quebec*, edited by Leslie Woodcock Tentler, 21–61. Washington, D.C.: Catholic University of America Press, 2007.

"Christians and Muslims: Working Together for Mankind's Spiritual Dimension." Vatican Insider Online. August 19, 2011, http://vaticaninsider.lastampa.it/en/world-news/detail/articolo/7190/.

Cleary, James F. "Catholic Participation in the World's Parliament of Religions, Chicago, 1893." *Catholic Historical Review* 55 (January 1970): 585–609.

Clifford, Catherine E. "Learning from the Council: A Church in Dialogue." *Theoforum* 44.1 (2013): 27–46.

Coleman, John A. "Vatican II as a Social Movement." In *The Belgian Contribution to the Second Vatican Council*, edited by D. Donnelly, J. Famerée, M. Lamberigts, and K. Schelkens, 5–28. Louvain, Belgium: Peeters, 2008.

"Collective Declaration of the German Hierarchy (1875)." In *The Christian Faith in the Doctrinal Documents of the Catholic Church*, 7th revised and enlarged edition, edited by Jacques Dupuis, nos. 840–41 (322). New York: Alba House, 2001.

Colson, J. *L'épiscopat catholique: Collégialité et primauté dans les trois premiers siècles de l'Église*. Paris: Cerf, 1963.

Congar, Yves. *L'Église de Saint Augustin à l'époque moderne*. Paris: Cerf, 1970.

———. *My Journal of the Council*. Edited by Denis Minns, and translated by Mary John Ronayne and Mary Cecily Boulding. Collegeville, Minn.: Liturgical Press, 2012.

Congregation for the Doctrine of the Faith. "Declaration on the Admission of Women to the Ministerial Priesthood." Papal Encyclicals, 15 October 1976. http://www.papalencyclicals.net/Paul06/p6interi.htm. 22 June 2013.

———. "Warning Regarding the Attempted Priestly Ordination of Some Catholic Women." In *The Papal 'No': A Comprehensive Guide to the Vatican's Rejection of Women's Ordination*, edited by Deborah Halter, 235. New York: Crossroad Publishing, 2004.

Connelly, John. *From Enemy to Brother: The Revolution in Catholic Teaching on the Jews, 1933–1965*. Cambridge, Mass., and London: Harvard University Press, 2012.

Conseil du Patrimoine Religieux du Québec. "2012–2013 budget appropriation for Québec religious heritage restoration," press release; "Restauration du patrimoine religieux: projets 2012–2013," press release.

Courteau, Joseph H. "Scènes d'autrefois et scènes d'aujourd'hui." In *La Croix du Chemin* edited by Louis-Athanase Fréchette, Camille Roy, Arthur Saint-Pierre, Édouard-Zotique Massicotte, and Jean-Baptiste Lagacé, 99–108. Montréal: Société Saint-Jean-Baptiste, 1941 [1915].

"Les croix de chemin à travers la patrie canadienne." *Le monde rural* (1943): 57–63.

Cummings, Kathleen Sprows, *New Women of the Old Faith: Gender and American Catholicism in the Progressive Era*. Chapel Hill: University of North Carolina Press, 2009.

Cuyler, Cornelius, S.S. "Perseverance Trends in the Seminary." *National Catholic Education Association Bulletin* 63 (Aug. 1966): 151–56.

Daniel, Norman. *Islam and the West: The Making of an Image*. Oxford: Oneworld, 2000. 1960 Reprint.

Denzinger, Heinrich J.D., and A. Schönmetzer, *Enchiridion Symbolorum, Definitionum et Declarationum de Rebus Fidei et Morum*. 32th ed. Barcinone: Herder, 1963.

Dillon, Michele, and Paul Wink. *In the Course of a Lifetime: Tracing Religious Belief, Practice and Change*. Berkeley: University of California Press, 2007.

Drolet, Jean-Claude. *L'Ordre des Chevaliers de Colomb*. Saguenay: Séminaire de Chicoutimi, 1968.

Dupuis, Jacques. "Notification on the book *Toward a Christian Theology of Religious Pluralism*." Vatican Online. http://www.vatican.va/roman_curia/congregations/cfaith/documents/rc_con_cfaith_doc_20010124_dupuis_en.html. 12 June 2013.

"Elections 2009: Indian Christians Demand a Place in Society." Asia News Online. 2 March 2009. http://www.asianews.it/news-en/Elections-2009:-Indian-Christians-demand-a-place-in-society-14620.html. 30 August 2012.

Faggioli, Massimo. *Vatican II: The Battle for Meaning*. New York and Mahwah, N.J.: Paulist Press, 2012.

———. "Vatican II: The History and the Narratives." *Theological Studies* 73 (2012): 749–67.

Famerée, Joseph, ed. *Vatican II comme style. L'herméneutique théologique du concile*. Unam Sanctam, N.S. 4. Paris: Cerf, 2012.

Farly, Viateur. "La croix du p'tit rocher." In *La Croix du Chemin*, edited by Louis-Athanase Fréchette, Camille Roy, Arthur Saint-Pierre, Édouard-Zotique Massicotte, and Jean-Baptiste Lagacé, 109–15. Montréal: Société Saint-Jean-Baptiste, 1941 [1915].

Fernando, Leonard, and George Gispert-Sauch. *Christianity in India: Two Thousand Years of Faith*. New Delhi and London: Penguin Viking, 2004.

Fisher, Eugene. "Catholics and Jews: Twenty Centuries and Counting." In *Examining Nostra Aetate after 40 Years: Catholic-Jewish Relations in Our Time*, edited by Anthony J. Cernera, 106–42. Fairfield, Conn.: Sacred Heart University Press, 2007.

Flannery, Edward H. *The Anguish of the Jews: Twenty-three Centuries of Anti-Semitism*. New York: Macmillan Co./London: Collier-Macmillan, 1965.

Forster, Gisela. "The Start: The Danube Seven and the Bishop Heroes." In *Women Find a Way: The Movement and Stories of Roman Catholic Womenpriests*, edited by Elsie Hainz McGrath, Bridget Mary Meehan, and Ida Raming, 9–13. College Station, Tex.: Virtualbookworm.com Publishing Inc., 2008.

Fries, Heinrich. *Fundamental Theology*. Translated by Robert J. Daly. Washington, D.C.: Catholic University of America Press, 1996.

Frisk, Jean M. "May, Mary's Month." University of Dayton Online. http://campus.udayton.edu/mary/meditations/crownmed.html?iframe=true&#top. 14 May 2013.

Gaillardetz, Richard R., *Teaching with Authority. A Theology of the Magisterium in the Church*. Theology and Life Series, 41. Collegeville, Minn.: Liturgical Press, 1997.

Gaillardetz, Richard R., and Catherine E. Clifford. *Keys to the Council: Unlocking the Teaching of Vatican II*. Collegeville, Minn.: Liturgical Press, 2012.

Gardiner, Anne Marie, ed. *Women and Catholic Priesthood: An Expanded Vision. Proceedings of the Detroit Ordination Conference*. New York: Paulist Press, 1976.

Gauthier, Lise, Normand St-André, and Jean-Marie Roy. *Nos Croix de Chemin: Notre héritage religieux et patrimonial*. Mascouche, PQ: Copie AM de Macouche, 2001.

Gauthier, Richard. "Autour du livre *Les églises du Québec. . . .*" In *Patrimoine et patrimonialisation du Québec et d'ailleurs*, edited by Martin Drouin, 203–8. Québec: Éditions MultiMondes, 2006.

Gibbons, James Cardinal. "The Needs of Humanity Supplied by the Catholic Religion." In *The Dawn of Religious Pluralism. Voices from the World's Parliament of Religions, 1893* edited by Richard Hughes Seager, 155–64. LaSalle, Ill.: Open Court, 1993.

Greeley, Andrew M. *The American Catholic: A Social Portrait*. New York: Basic Books, 1977.

———. "Popular Devotions: Friend or Foe?" *Worship* 33 (Oct. 1959): 569–673.

Grootaers, Jan, ed. *Primauté et collegialité: Le dossier de Gérard Philips sur la Nota Explicativa Praevia (Lumen Gentium, Chap. III). Présenté avec introduction historique, annotations et annexes*, Bibliotheca Ephemeridum Theologicarum Lovaniensium, 72. Louvain: Peeters, 1986.

Groulx, Jocelyn. "Préface: Des défis collectifs face au patrimoine religieux." In *Le Patrimoine religieux du* Québec, edited by Solange Lefebvre, 17–19. Québec: Presses de l'Université Laval, 2009.

Groupe des Dombes. *One Teacher: Doctrinal Authority in the Church*. Translated by Catherine E. Clifford. Grand Rapids: Wm. B. Eerdmans, 2010.

Guitton, Jean. *The Church and the Laity: From Newman to Vatican II*. New York: Alba House, 1965.

———. *Dialogues avec Paul VI*. Fayard, 1967.

Haight, Father Roger. "Notification on the book *Jesus Symbol of God*." Vatican Online. http://www.vatican.va/roman_curia/congregations/cfaith/documents/rc_con_cfaith_doc_20041213_notification-fr-haight_en.html. 12 June 2013.

Halter, Deborah, ed. *The Papal 'No': A Comprehensive Guide to the Vatican's Rejection of Women's Ordination*. New York: Crossroad Publishing, 2004.

Hebblethwaite, Peter. *John XXIII: Pope of the Century*. London and New York: Continuum, 2000.

———. *John XXIII, Pope of the Council*. London: Geoffrey Chapman, 1984.

Hegy, Pierre, and Joseph Martos, eds. *Catholic Divorce: The Deception of Annulments*. New York, Continuum, 2000.

Heinz, Hanspeter. "Your Privilege: You Have Jewish Friends: Michael Signer's Hermeneutics of Friendship." In *Christ Jesus and the Jewish People Today: New Explorations of Theological Interrelationships*, edited by Philip A. Cunningham et al., 1–13. Grand Rapids, Mich., and Cambridge, UK: William B. Eerdmans Publishing Co.; Rome: Gregorian & Biblical Press, 2011.

Heinzelmann, Gertrud, ed. *Wir schweigen nicht langer! Frauen aussern sich zum II Vatikanischen Konzil*. Zürich: Interfeminas-Verlag, 1964.

Henold, Mary J. *Catholic and Feminist: The Surprising History of the American Catholic Feminist Movement*. Chapel Hill: University of North Carolina Press, 2008.

Hötzel, Norbert. *Die Uroffenbarung im französischen Traditionalismus*. Munich: M. Hueber, 1962.

International Council of Christians and Jews. *A Time for Recommitment: Jewish Christian Dialogue 70 Years after War and Shoah*. Berlin: Konrad-Adenauer-Stiftung, 2009.

Isaac, Jules. *The Teaching of Contempt: Christian Roots of Anti-Semitism*, translated by Helen Weaver. New York: Holt, Rinehart and Winston, 1964.

———. *Jesus and Israel*, edited by Claire Huchet Bishop and translated by Sally Gran. New York: Holt, Rinehart and Winston, 1971.

Jaspers, Karl. *The Origin and Goal of History*. Translated by Michael Bullock. New Haven, Conn.: Yale University Press.

Joly, Diane. "Des croix de chemin en quête de protecteurs." *Rabaska* 6 (2008): 41–67.

Kane, Paula. "American Catholic Studies at a Crossroads." *Religion and American Culture* 16.2 (2006): 263–71.

Karlsson, Bengt G. "Entering into the Christian Dharma: Contemporary 'Tribal' Conversions in India." In *Christians, Cultural Interactions, and India's Religious Traditions*, edited by Judith M. Brown and Robert Eric Frykenberg, 133–53. Grand Rapids, Mich.: William B. Eerdmans Publishing Co.; London: RoutledgeCurzon, 2002.

Kairos Palestine (Organization). *Kairos Palestine: A Moment of Truth*. Jerusalem, December 15, 2009.

Keegan, Patrick. "Address of Mr. Patrick Keegan, On Behalf of the Auditors, to the Fathers of the Second Vatican Council," Cardijn Pioneers. http://pioneers .josephcardijn.com/address-to-vatican-ii. 18 June 2013.

Kelly, Timothy. *The Transformation of American Catholicism: The Pittsburgh Laity and the Second Vatican Council, 1950–1972*. Notre Dame, Ind.: University of Notre Dame Press, 2009.

Kenny, Anthony J. *Catholics, Jews, and the State of Israel*. New York and Mahwah, N.J.: Stimulus Book/Paulist Press, 1993.

Kobler, John F. *Vatican II and Phenomenology: Reflections on the Life-World of the Church*. Dordrecht and Boston: Martinus Nijhoff Publishers, 1985.

Komonchak, Joseph A. "Novelty in Continuity." *America*, 2 February 2009. americamagazine.org/issue/684/article/novelty-continuity. 22 June 2013.

Küng, Hans, Yves Congar, and Daniel O'Hanlon, eds. *Council Speeches of Vatican II*. Glen Rock, N.J.: Paulist, 1964.

Lafont, Ghislain. *Imagining the Catholic Church: Structured Communion in the Spirit*. Translated by John J. Burkhard. Collegeville, Minn.: Liturgical Press, 2000. [Original version: *Imaginer l'Église catholique*. Paris: Cerf, 1995.]

Lamberigts, Mathijs, and Leo Declerck. "The Role of Cardinal Léon-Joseph Suenens at Vatican II." In *The Belgian Contribution to the Second Vatican Council*, edited by D. Donnelly, J. Famerée, M. Lamberigts, and K. Schelkens. 61–217. Bibliotheca Ephemeridum Theologicarum Lovaniensium, 216. Leuven: Peeters, 2008.

Lamberigts, Mathijs, and Leo Kenis, eds. *Vaticanum II: Geschiedenis of inspiratie? Theologische opstellen over het tweede Vaticaans concilie*. Antwerp: Halewijn, 2013.

"Lay Auditors at the Second Vatican Council." Pontifical Council for the Laity. http://www.laici.va/content/laici/en/media/notizie/gli-uditori-laici-al-concilio-vaticano-ii.html. 18 June 2013.

Lefebvre, J. H. *Christophe Colomb et l'Ordre des Chevaliers de Colomb*. N.p.: Éditions Christophe Colomb, 1972.

Lefebvre, Solange. "Introduction." In *Le patrimoine religieux du* Québec, edited by Solange Lefebvre, 19–34. Québec: Presses de l'Université Laval, 2009.

Léger, Paul-Émile Cardinal. "Lettre inédite du Cardinal Paul-Émile Léger au Pape Jean XXIII en août 1962." In *Mémoires de Vatican II*, edited by Brigitte Caulier and Gilles Routhier, 93–113. Montréal: Fides, 1997.

Le Guillou, M. J. "Le parallélisme entre le Collège apostolique et le Collège épiscopal." *Istina* 10 (1964): 103–10.

Lesegretain, Claire. "Jean Guitton, premier laïc à parler au concile." In *Croire. Questions de vie, questions de foi* (8 October 2002). http://www.croire.com/Definitions/Vie-chretienne/Vatican-II/La-voix-des-laics/Jean-Guitton. 28 September 2013.

Lucier, Pierre. "La Révolution tranquille: Quelle sortie de religion? Sortie de quelle religion?" In *Modernité et religion au Québec: Où en sommes-nous?*, edited by Robert Mager, Serge Cantin, Maxime Allard, et al., 11–26. Québec: Presses de l'Université Laval, 2010.

Lyotard, Jean-François. *La condition postmoderne. Rapport sur le savoir*. Paris: Les Éditions de Minuit, 1979. Reprint 2013.

Madges, William, and Michael J. Daley, eds. *Vatican II: Fifty Personal Stories*. Maryknoll, New York: Orbis, 2012.

Mager, Robert, and Serge Cantin. "Introduction: Religion, modernité, Québec." In *Modernité et religion au Québec: Où en sommes-nous?*, edited by Robert Mager, Serge Cantin, Maxime Allard, et al., 7–10. Québec: PUL, 2010.

Magister, Sandro. "The Council in the Intimate Thoughts of Pope John XXIII." Chiesa. http://chiesa.espresso.repubblica.it/articolo/1350349?eng=y. 18 June 2013.

Maheu, Marie-Eve. "L'histoire oubliée des croix de chemin." Radio-Canada, 29 March 2013. http://blogues.radio-canada.ca/rive-sud/2013/03/29/croix-de-chemin-patrimoine/. 4 April 2013.

Martin, Dale. *Sex and the Single Savior: Gender and Sexuality in Biblical Interpretation.* Louisville: Westminster John Knox, 2006.

Martin, Hervé. "La fonction polyvalente des croix à la fin du Moyen-Âge." *Annales de Bretagne et des pays de l'Ouest* 90.2 (1983): 295–310.

Martinez, Franciso Javier. "Eastern Christian Apocalyptic in the Early Muslim Period: Pseudo-Methodius and Pseudo-Athanasius." Ph.D. diss., Catholic University of America, 1985.

Massicotte, Édouard-Zotique. "Avant-Propos." In *La Croix du Chemin* edited by Louis-Athanase Fréchette, Camille Roy, Arthur Saint-Pierre, Édouard-Zotique Massicotte, and Jean-Baptiste Lagacé, 21–24. Montréal: Société Saint-Jean-Baptiste, 1941 [1915].

Maximos IV Saigh, Patriarch of the Melkites. "The Supreme Senate of the Catholic Church." In *Council Speeches of Vatican II*, edited by Hans Küng, Yves Congar, and Daniel O'Hanlon, 133–37. Glen Rock, N.J.: Paulist, 1964.

May, Melanie A. *Jerusalem Testament: Palestinian Christians Speak, 1988–2008.* Grand Rapids, Mich.: William B. Eerdmans Publishing Co., 2010.

Mayr-Lumetzberger, Christine. "Reflections on My Way: God's Call to Me." In *Women Find a Way: The Movement and Stories of Roman Catholic Womenpriests*, edited by Elsie Hainz McGrath, Bridget Mary Meehan, and Ida Raming, 14–18. College Station, Tex.: Virtualbookworm.com Publishing Inc., 2008.

McCartin, James P. *Prayers of the Faithful: The Shifting Spiritual Life of American Catholics.* Cambridge, Mass.: Harvard University Press, 2011.

McDannell, Colleen. *Material Christianity: Religion and Popular Culture in America.* New Haven: Yale University Press, 1995.

———. *The Spirit of Vatican II: A History of Catholic Reform in America.* New York: Basic Books, 2011.

McEnroy, Carmen. *Guests in Their Own House: The Women of Vatican II.* New York: Crossroad, 1996.

McGinn, Bernard. *Antichrist: Two Thousand Years of the Human Fascination with Evil.* San Francisco: HarperSanFranciso, 1994.

McGrath, Elsie Hainz. "The Road Less Traveled By." In *Women Find a Way: The Movement and Stories of Roman Catholic Womenpriests*, edited by Elsie Hainz McGrath, Bridget Mary Meehan, and Ida Raming, 108–14. College Station, Tex.: Virtualbookworm.com Publishing Inc., 2008.

McGreevy, John T. *Parish Boundaries: The Catholic Encounter with Race in the Twentieth-Century Urban North.* Chicago: University of Chicago Press, 1996.

Meehan, Bridget Mary. "Roman Catholic Womenpriests: Vision and Mission." *YouTube*, 29 August 2007. http://www.youtube.com/watch?v=cJrn-rmHpPQ. 22 June 2013.

———. "Roman Catholic Women Priests Invite You to Stand with Fr. Roy Bourgeois to Resist Vatican Oppression and to Proclaim Equality for Women in the Church." *Bridget Mary's Blog*, 6 April 2011. http://bridgetmarys.blogspot.com/2011/04/association-of-roman-catholic-women.html. 22 June 2013.

Meehan, Bridget Mary, Olivia Doku, and Victoria Rue. "A Brief Overview of Womenpriests in the History of the Roman Catholic Church." *Roman Catholic Womenpriests*, http://www.romancatholicwomenpriests.org/resources_links.htm. 22 June 2013.

Meunier, E. M., J. F. Laniel, and J. C. Demers, "Permanence et recomposition de la 'Religion Culturelle.'" In *Modernité et religion au Québec: Où en sommes-nous?*, edited by Robert Mager, Serge Cantin, Maxime Allard, et al., 79–128. Québec: Presses de l'Université Laval, 2010.

Moorman, John. *Vatican Observed: An Anglican Impression of Vatican II*. London: Darton, Longman & Todd, 1967.

Morisset, Lucie K. "Une île, un zoo, une ville." In *Patrimoine: sources et paradoxes de l'identité*, edited by Jean-Yves, 142–86. Rennes, France: Presses Universitaires de Rennes, 2011.

Morselli, Marco. "Jules Isaac and the Origins of *Nostra Aetate*." In *Nostra Aetate: Origins, Promulgation, Impact on Jewish-Catholic Relations*, edited by Neville Lamdan and Alberto Melloni, *Christianity and History*, vol. 5, 21–28. Berlin: Lit Verlag, 2007.

Müller, Iris. "My Story, Condensed." In *Women Find a Way: The Movement and Stories of Roman Catholic Womenpriests*, edited by Elsie Hainz McGrath, Bridget Mary Meehan, and Ida Raming, 19–20. College Station, Tex.: Virtualbookworm. com Publishing Inc., 2008.

Murray, John Courtney. *We Hold These Truths: Catholic Reflections on the American Proposition*. New York: Sheed and Ward, 1960.

———. *Religious Liberty: Catholic Struggles with Pluralism*, edited by J. Leon Hooper. Louisville: Westminster John Knox Press, 1993.

Neuner, Josef, and Jacques Dupuis, eds. *The Christian Faith in the Doctrinal Documents of the Catholic Church*. 7th revised and enlarged edition, edited by J. Dupuis. New York: Alba House, 2001.

Nicholls, William. *Christian Antisemitism: A History of Hate*. Northvale, N.J., and London: Jason Aronson, 1993.

Nirenberg, David. *Anti-Judaism: The Western Tradition*. New York: W. W. Norton & Co., 2013.

Nugent, Robert. *Silence Speaks: Teilhard de Chardin, Yves Congar, John Courtney Murray, and Thomas Merton*. Mahwah, N.J.: Paulist Press, 2011.

O'Brien, David J. *The Renewal of American Catholicism*. New York: Paulist Press, 1972.

O'Collins, Gerald. "Does Vatican II Represent Continuity or Discontinuity?" *Theological Studies* 73 (2012): 268–94.

———. *The Second Vatican Council on Other Religions*. Oxford: Oxford University Press, 2013.

O'Malley, John W. "Trent and Vatican II: Two Styles of Church." In *From Trent to Vatican II: Historical and Theological Investigations*, edited by Raymond F. Bulman and Frederick J. Parrella, 301–20. Oxford: Oxford University Press, 2006.

———. "Vatican II: Did Anything Happen?" *Theological Studies* 67 (2006): 3–33. Also in *Vatican II: Did Anything Happen?*, edited by David G. Schultenover, 52–91. New York: Continuum, 2007.

———. *What Happened at Vatican II*. Cambridge, Mass.: Belknap Press of Harvard University Press, 2008.

———. "'The Hermeneutic of Reform': A Historical Analysis." *Theological Studies* 73.3 (2012): 517–46.

O'Toole, James M. "In the Court of Conscience: American Catholics and Confession, 1900–1975." In *Habits of Devotion: Catholic Religious Practice in Twentieth-Century America*, edited by James M. O'Toole, 131–85. Ithaca, N.Y.: Cornell University Press, 2004.

O'Toole, James M., ed. *Habits of Devotion: Catholic Religious Practice in Twentieth Century America*. Ithaca, N.Y.: Cornell University Press, 2004.

Oesterreicher, John M. "Declaration on the Relationship of the Church to Non-Christian Religions: Introduction and Commentary." In *Commentary on the Documents of Vatican II*, vol. III, *Declaration on the Relationship of the Church to Non-Christian Religions; Dogmatic Constitution on Divine Revelation; Decree on the Apostolate of the Laity*, edited by Herbert Vorgrimler, 1–136. New York: Herder and Herder, 1969.

Orsi, Robert. "'The Infant of Prague's Nightie': The Devotional Origins of Contemporary Catholic Memory." *U.S. Catholic Historian* 21.2 (2003): 1–18.

Ouellet, Paul-André. *Les Croix de Chemin dans la MRC les Basques*. Trois-Pistoles: Société d'histoire de Trois-Pistoles, 2010.

Outler, Albert. *Methodist Observer at Vatican II*. Westminster, Md.: Newman Press, 1967.

Palmer, Andrew, and Sebastian Brock, trans. *The Apocalypse of Pseudo-Methodius*. In *The Seventh Century in the West-Syrian Chronicles*, edited by Andrew Palmer, 222–42. Translated Texts for Historians, 15. Liverpool: Liverpool University Press, 1993.

Parent, Frédéric. "Dieu, le capitalisme et le développement local: Étude monographique d'un village québécois." Ph.D. diss., Université de Montréal, 2009.

———. "Pratique religieuse et espaces-temps sociaux dans un village québécois." In *Modernité et religion au Québec: Où en sommes-nous?*, edited by Robert Mager, Serge Cantin, Maxime Allard, et al., 181–93. Québec: Presses de l'Université Laval, 2010.

Philips, Gérard. "Deux tendances dans la théologie contemporaine." *Nouvelle Revue Theologique* 85.3 (1963): 225–38.

———. "History of the Constitution." In *Commentary on the Documents of Vatican II*, vol. I, edited by Herbert Vorgrimler, 105–37. New York: Herder and Herder, 1966.

Pieper, Josef. *Tradition als Herausforderung*. Munich: Kösel Verlag, 1963.

"Pontiff in Blue mosque." YouTube. http://www.youtube.com/watch?v=OZQu1t7RXUA; http://news.bbc.co.uk/2/hi/europe/6158811.stm. 12 June 2013.

Pontifical Council for Interreligious Dialogue. "Christians and Hindus: Together in Promoting Religious Freedom." Vatican Online. 2011. http://www.vatican .va/roman_curia/pontifical_councils/interelg/documents/rc_pc_interelg_ doc_20111020_diwali_en.html. 12 June 2013.

Pope Benedict XVI. "Post-Synodal Apostolic Exhortation *Ecclesia in Medio Oriente*." Vatican Online. http://www.vatican.va/holy_father/benedict_xvi/ apost_exhortations/documents /hf_ben-xvi_exh_20120914_ecclesia-in-medio-oriente_en.pdf. 11 June 2013.

———. "Faith, Reason and the University: Memories and Reflections." Vatican Online. http://www.vatican.va/holy_father/benedict_xvi/speeches/2006/september/documents/hf_ben-xvi_spe_20060912_university-regensburg_en.html. 12 June 2013.

———. "Post-Synodal Apostolic Exhortation *Ecclesia in Medio Oriente.*" Vatican Online. http://www.vatican.va/holy_father/benedict_xvi/apost_exhortations/documents/hf_ben-xvi_exh_20120914_ecclesia-in-medio-oriente_en.html. 14 September 2012.

———. "Homily, Ordinary Public Consistory for the Creation of New Cardinals, 25 November 2007." Vatican Online. http://www.vatican.va/holy_father/benedict_xvi/homilies/2007/documents/hf_ben-xvi_hom_20071125_anello-cardinalizio_en.html. 22 June 2013.

———. *Theological Highlights of Vatican II*. Mahwah, N.J.: Paulist Press, 2009.

Pope Francis. "Apostolic Exhortation on the Joy of the Gospel (*Evangelii Gaudium*)." Vatican Online. http://www.vatican.va/evangelii-gaudium/en/. 12 August 2014.

———. "The Message of Pope Francis to Muslims throughout the World for the End of Ramadan ('Id al-Fitr), 10 July 2013." Vatican Online. http://www.vatican.va/holy_father/francesco/messages/pont-messages/2013/documents/papa-francesco_20130710_musulmani-ramadan_en.html. 4 February 2015.

Pope Gregory XVI. "*Mirari Vos*: On Liberalism and Religious Indifferentism, Encyclical." Papal Encyclicals Online. http://www.papalencyclicals.net/Greg16/g16mirar.htm# par13. 11 June 2013.

Pope John XXIII. *Humanae Salutis* (Convocation of the Second Vatican Council, December 25, 1961). In *The Documents of Vatican II*, edited by Walter M. Abbott, 703–9. New York: America Press, 1966.

———. Radio address of September 11, 1962. For the text of this speech: *Acta Apostolicae Sedis* 54 (1962): 678–85.

———. "Opening Speech to the Vatican II Council." *St. Michael's Call: Papal Library*. http://www.saint-mike.org/library/papal_library/johnxxiii/opening_speech_vaticanii.html. 11 June 2013.

———. "Pope John's Opening Speech to the Council, [Gaudet Mater Ecclesia]." In *The Documents of Vatican II*, edited by Walter M. Abbott, 710–19. New York: America Press, 1966.

———. "*Pacem in Terris*, Encyclical of Pope John XXIII on Establishing Universal Peace in Truth, Justice, Charity, and Liberty." Vatican Online. http://www.vatican.va/holy_father/john_xxiii/encyclicals/documents/hf_j-xxiii_enc_11041963_pacem_en.html. 18 June 2013.

Pope John Paul II. "The Challenge and the Possibility of Peace." *Origins* 16/21 (Nov. 6, 1986): 370.

———. "*Ordinatio Sacerdotalis*" ("On Reserving Priestly Ordination to Men Alone"). Vatican Online. http://www.vatican.va/holy_father/john_paul_ii/apost_letters/documents/hf_jp-ii_apl_22051994_ordinatio-sacerdotalis_en.html. 22 June 2013

———. *Redemptoris Missio*. Vatican Online. http://www.vatican.va/holy_father/john_paul_ii/encyclicals/documents/hf_jp-ii_enc_07121990_redemptoris-missio_en.html. 12 June 2013.

———. "Message to the Faithful of Islam at the End of the Month of Ramadan, April 3, 1991." In *John Paul II and Interreligious Dialogue*, edited by Byron L. Sherwin and Harold Kasimow. Maryknoll, N.Y.: Orbis Books, 1999.

———. "Tertio Millennio Adveniente." Vatican Online. http://www.vatican.va/holy_father/john_paul_ii/apost_letters/documents/hf_jp-ii_apl_10111994_tertio-millennio-adveniente_en.html. 11 June 2013.

———. *Crossing the Threshold of Hope*. Edited by Vittorio Messori, and translated by Jenny McPhee and Martha McPhee. New York: A. A. Knopf, 1994.

———. "Address of the Holy Father: Meeting with the Muslim Leaders, Omayyad Great Mosque, Damascus." Vatican Online. http://www.vatican.va/holy_father/john_paul_ii/speeches/2001/documents/hf_jp-ii_spe_20010506_omayyadi_en.html. 11 June 2013.

———. "*Apostolos Suos*: On the Theological and Juridical Nature of Episcopal Conferences (1)." Vatican Online. http://www.vatican.va/holy_father/john_paul_ii/motu_proprio/documents/hf_jp-ii_motu-proprio_22071998_apostolos-suos_en.html. 22 June 2013

———. "Pope Makes Turkish Mosque Visit." BBC News Online. http://news.bbc.co.uk/2/hi/europe/6158811.stm. 14 September 2012.

Pope Paul VI. "*Ecclesiam Suam*, Encyclical of Pope Paul VI on The Church." Vatican Online. http://www.vatican.va/holy_father/paul_vi/encyclicals/documents/hf_p-vi_enc_06081964_ecclesiam_en.html. 18 June 2013.

———. *Motu proprio Apostolica Sollicitudo*, September 15, 1965, *AAS* 57 (1965) 794–804.

Pope Pius IX. "Apostolic Brief of March 6, 1875." In *The Christian Faith in the Doctrinal Documents of the Catholic Church*, 7th revised and enlarged edition, edited by Jacques Dupuis, no 840 (322). New York: Alba House, 2001.

Pope, Stephen J., and Charles Hefling, eds. *Dominus Iesus*. In *Sic et Non: Encountering Dominus Iesus*, 3–26. Maryknoll, N.Y.: Orbis Books, 2002.

Racine, Jacques. "École Québécoise, modernité et religion." In *Modernité et religion au Québec: Où en sommes-nous?*, edited by Robert Mager, Serge Cantin, Maxime Allard, et al, 277–91. Québec: Presses de l'Université Laval, 2010.

Rahner, Karl. "Basic Theological Interpretation of the Second Vatican Council." *Theological Investigations*, 20. London: Darton, Longman & Todd, 1981.

———. "Dogmatic Constitution on the Church: Chapter III, Articles 18–27." In *Commentary on the Documents of Vatican II*, vol. I, edited by Herbert Vorgrimler, 186–217. New York: Herder and Herder, 1966.

Raming, Ida. "Situation of Women in the Roman Catholic Church: Canonical Background and Perspective." In *Women Find a Way: The Movement and Stories of Roman Catholic Womenpriests*, edited by Elsie Hainz McGrath, Bridget Mary Meehan, and Ida Raming, 21–26. College Station, Tex.: Virtualbookworm.com Publishing Inc., 2008.

Raming, Ida, and Iris Müller. "Gertrud Heinzelmann." Ministry for Women. http://www.ministryforwomen.org/called/heinzelm.asp. 22 June 2013.

Ratzinger, Joseph. *Theological Highlights of Vatican II*. New York: Paulist Press, 1999.

Reinders, Eric. *Borrowed Gods and Foreign Bodies: Christian Missionaries Imagine Chinese Religion*. Berkeley, Calif.: University of California Press, 2004.

Robinson, Rowena and Joseph Marianus Kujur. "Introduction." In *Margins of Faith: Dalit and Tribal Christianity in India*, edited by Rowena Robinson and Joseph Marianus Kujur, 1–28. Los Angeles: Sage Publications, 2010.

Roman Catholic Womenpriests—North America. "Vision Statement." *Roman Catholic Womenpriests*, 3 February 2007. http://romancatholicwomenpriests.org/constitution.htm. 22 June 2013.

——. "RCWP call on Pope to lift Excommunications." *Roman Catholic Womenpriests*, 28 January 2009. http://romancatholicwomenpriests.org/press_releases/pressrelease10.htm. 22 June 2013.

——. "RCWP FAQs: True and False about Women's Ordinations." Roman Catholic Womenpriests. http://www.romancatholicwomenpriests.org/faq.htm. 22 June 2013.

——. "Roman Catholic Womenpriests' Response to Vatican Decrees of Excommunication," http://romancatholicwomenpriests.org/archivepressreleases .htm. 23 April 2014.

Routhier, Gilles. "Les réactions du cardinal Léger à la préparation de Vatican II." *Revue d'histoire de l'Église de France* 80.204 (1994): 281–302.

Roy, Camille. "Préface." In *La Croix du Chemin*, edited by Louis-Athanase Fréchette, Camille Roy, Arthur Saint-Pierre, Édouard-Zotique Massicotte, and Jean-Baptiste Lagacé, 11–14. Montréal: Société Saint-Jean-Baptiste, 1941 [1915].

Rymarz, Richard. "Forward Thinking." *Compass* 44.2 (Winter 2010): 1–2.

Rush, Ormond. *Still Interpreting Vatican II: Some Hermeneutical Principles*. New York and Mahwah, N.J.: Paulist Press, 2004.

Saint-Pierre, Arthur. "Introduction." In *La Croix du Chemin*, edited by Louis-Athanase Fréchette, Camille Roy, Arthur Saint-Pierre, Édouard-Zotique Massicotte, and Jean-Baptiste Lagacé, 15–20. Montréal: Société Saint-Jean-Baptiste, 1941 [1915].

Saint Therese of Lisieux. *Story of a Soul: The Autobiography of St. Thérèse of Lisieux*. Translated by John C Clark, OCD, 2nd edition. Washington, D.C.: ICS Publications, 1976.

Saldahna, Shirley, et al. "American Catholics—Ten Years Later." *The Critic* 33 (January—February 1975): 13–21.

Schiller, Gertrud. *Iconography of Christian Art*, vol. 2. London: Lund Humphries, 1971.

Schloeder, Steven. *Architecture in Communion: Implementing the Second Vatican Council through Liturgy and Architecture*. San Francisco: Ignatius Press 1998.

Schloesser, Stephen. "Against Forgetting: Memory, History, Vatican II," *Theological Studies* 67 (2006): 275–319. Also in *Vatican II: Did Anything Happen?*, edited by David G. Schultenover, 92–152. New York: Continuum, 2007.

Second Extraordinary Synod. "The Final Report: Synod of Bishops." *Origins* 15 (December 19, 1985): 444–50.

Sekhar, Vincent. *Building Strong Neighbourhoods: Religion and Politics in Secular India*. Bangalore, India: Claretian Publications, 2008.

Sharma, Ritu. "Mob Attacks Christians for Playing Hymns: Religious Tensions Grow in Maharashtra." UCalif.NEWS Online. 16 January 2013. http://www.ucanews .com/news/mob-attacks-christians-for-playing-hymns/67128. 16 January 2013.

Simard, Jean. *Le Québec pour terrain: Itinéraire d'un missionnaire du patrimoine religieux*. Québec: Presses de l'Université Laval, 2004.

Simard, Jean, and Jocelyne Milot. *Les croix de chemin du Québec: Inventaire sélectif et trésor*. Québec: Ministère de la Culture et Communications, 1994.

Simard, Jean, Jocelyne Milot, and René Bouchard. *Un patrimoine méprisé: la religion populaire des Québécois*. Montreal: Hurtubise, 1979.

Shofany, Saba. *The Melkites at the Vatican Council II: Contribution of the Melkite Prelates to Vatican Council II*. Bloomington, Ind.: Authorhouse, 2005.

Stanley, D. M. "The New Testament Basis for the Concept of Collegiality." *Theological Studies* 25 (1964): 197–216.

Stransky, Thomas. "The Observers at Vatican Two: A Unique Experience of Dialogue." *Bulletin Centro Pro Unione* 63 (Spring 2002): 8–14.

———. "The Genesis of *Nostra Aetate*: Surprises, Setbacks, and Blessings." *America*, 4 October 2005, 8–12.

———"The Genesis of *Nostra Aetate*: An Insider's Story." In *Nostra Aetate: Origins, Promulgation, Impact on Jewish-Catholic Relations*, edited by Neville Lamdan and Alberto Melloni, Christianity and History, vol. 5, 29–53. Berlin: Lit Verlag, 2007.

Suenens, Joseph Cardinal. "Aux origines du concile Vatican II." *Nouvelle Revue Théologique* 107 (1985): 3–21. [English translation: "A Plan for the Whole Council." In *Vatican II by those Who Were There*, edited by Alberic Stacpoole, 88–105. London: G. Chapman, 1986.]

———. *Souvenirs et espérances*. Paris: Fayard, 1991.

Sugrue, Thomas J. *The Origins of the Urban Crisis: Race and Inequality in Postwar Detroit*. Princeton: Princeton University Press, 1996.

Swidler, Leonard, and Arlene Swidler, eds. *Women Priests: A Catholic Commentary on the Vatican Declaration*. New York: Paulist Press, 1977.

Tanner, Norman P. *The Church and the World: Gaudium et Spes, Inter Mirifica*. New York and Mahwah, N.J.: Paulist Press, 2005.

———, ed. *Decrees of the Ecumenical Councils*. 2 vols. (London: Sheed & Ward and Washington, D.C.: Georgetown University Press, 1990).

———. *Vatican II: The Essential Texts*. New York: Image Books, 2012.

Teltumbde, Anand, ed. *Hindutva and Dalits: Perspectives for Understanding Communal Praxis*. Kolkata, India: Samya, 2005.

Tentler, Leslie Woodcock. *Seasons of Grace: A History of the Catholic Archdiocese of Detroit*. Detroit: Wayne State University Press, 1990.

———. *Catholics and Contraception: An American History*. Ithaca, N.Y.: Cornell University Press, 2004.

Timmermann, Achim. "Highways to Heaven (and Hell): Wayside Crosses and the Making of Late Medieval Landscape." In *The Authority of the Word, Reflecting on Image and Text in Northern Europe, 1400–1800*, edited by Celeste Brusati et. al., 385–442. Leiden: Brill, 2011.

Turgeon, Laurier, and Louise Saint-Pierre. "Building an Integrated Multimedia Digital Database . . ." In *Spirit of Place: Between Tangible and Intangible Heritage*, edited by Laurier Turgeon, 411–28. Québec: Presses de l'Université Laval, 2009.

Vatican II—The Voice of the Church. "The Church's English Voice—Bishop Christopher Butler, OSB." The Voice of the Church. http://vatican2voice .org/4basics/papal.htm. 22 June 2013.

Vorgrimler, Herbert, ed. *Commentary on the Documents of Vatican II*. 5 vols. New York: Herder and Herder, 1966.

Wallace, Ruth A. *They Call Her Pastor: A New Role for Catholic Women*. Albany: SUNY Press, 1992.

Wilkins, John. "Bishops or Branch Managers?" *Commonweal* (October 12, 2012): 16–21.

———. "From peritus to pope: the causes of Ratzinger's about-face." *National Catholic Reporter*, 11 October 2012, 17, 19.

Witherup, Ronald D. *Scripture: Dei Verbum,* Rediscovering Vatican II Series. New York. Mahwah, N.J.; Paulist Press, 2006.

Women's Ordination Conference. "Our Story." Women's Ordination Conference. http://www.womensordination.org/content/view/8/59/. 22 June 2013.

———. "Top Ten Reasons to Ordain Women." Women's Ordination Conference. http:// www.womensordination.org/content/view/241/. 22 June 2013.

Womenpriests. "Home page." Womenpriests http://www.womenpriests.org. 22 June 2013.

# Contributors

CATHERINE E. CLIFFORD (Ph.D., University of St. Michael's College, Toronto) is a professor in theology at Saint Paul University in Ottawa, Canada, and a founding member of the Research Centre for Vatican II and Twenty-First Century Catholicism. She has authored several books, including *Decoding Vatican II: Interpretation and Ongoing Reception* (Mahwah, N.J.: Paulist Press, 2014), *The Groupe des Dombes: A Dialogue of Conversion* (New York: Peter Lang, 2005), and *Keys to the Council: Unlocking the Teaching of Vatican II* (Collegeville, Minn.: Liturgical Press, 2012), coauthored with Richard R. Gaillardetz. She edited *Groupe des Dombes. For the Communion of the Churches* (Grand Rapids, Mich.: Eerdmans, 2010) and *A Century of Prayer for Christian Unity* (Grand Rapids, Mich.: Eerdmans, 2009). With Michael Attridge and Gilles Routhier, she coedited *Vatican II: Expériences canadiennes/ Canadian Experiences* (Ottawa: University of Ottawa Press, 2011).

HILLARY KAELL (Ph.D., Harvard University) is an assistant professor in the Department of Religion at Concordia University in Montreal, Canada. Her scholarship focuses on North American Christian practice and material culture. Her monograph *Walking Where Jesus Walked: American Christians and Holy Land Pilgrimage* (New York: New York University Press, 2014) is the first major study of U.S. Christian trips to Israel-Palestine. She is currently working on a second book about Christian child-sponsorship programs and editing a volume tentatively titled "Religious Lives and Landscapes in Contemporary Quebec," to be published by McGill-Queen's University Press.

LEO D. LEFEBURE (Ph.D., University of Chicago) is the Matteo Ricci Professor of Theology at Georgetown University, Washington, D.C. He is actively involved in the Catholic interreligious dialogue with Jews, Muslims, Buddhists, and, more recently, with Hindus. His major book publications include *Toward a Contemporary Wisdom Christology: A Study of Karl Rahner and Norman Pittenger* (Lanham, Md.: University Press of America, 1988), *Life Transformed: Meditations on the Christian Scriptures in Light of Buddhist Perspectives* (Chicago: ACTA Publications, 1989), and *True and Holy: Christian Scripture and Other Religions* (Maryknoll, N.Y.: Orbis Books, 2013). With Peter Feldmeier he coauthored *The Path of Wisdom: A Christian Commentary on the Dhammapada* (Grand Rapids, Mich.: Eerdmans, 2011), which was the recipient of the 2011 Frederick J. Streng Book of the Year Award from the Society for Buddhist-Christian Studies. His other volumes include *The Buddha and the Christ: Explorations in Buddhist-Christian Dialogue* (Maryknoll, N.Y.: Orbis Books, 1993) and *Revelation, the Religions, and Violence* (Maryknoll, N.Y.: Orbis Books, 2000), for which he received the Pax Christi U.S.A. 2001 Book Award.

SAM MIGLARESE (S.T.L., Gregorian University, and S.T.D., University of St. Thomas Aquinas, both in Rome) is an adjunct instructor in the Department of Religious Studies and in the Program in Education at Duke University, North Carolina. His main field of interest is the history and reception of the Second Vatican Council. His doctoral dissertation focused on the ministry of the Word at the Council, its meaning and implications of the priest's *primum officium* as proclaimer of the Word. From 1990 to 1995 he led a Diocesan Synod for the Diocese of Charleston, South Carolina, that replicated at a local level the vision and process of the Second Vatican Council. He also directs the Duke-Durham Neighborhood Partnership and serves as the director of community engagement for the Office of Durham and Regional Affairs at Duke University. He also is an associate pastor at First Presbyterian Church, Durham, North Carolina.

DAVID MORGAN (Ph.D., University of Chicago) is a professor of religion and the chair of the Department of Religious Studies at Duke University in Durham, North Carolina. His area of work is the visual and material cultures of modern Christianity. His major publications include *Visual Piety* (Berkeley: University of California Press, 1998), *Protestants and Pictures* (New York: Oxford University Press, 1999), *The Sacred Gaze* (Berkeley: University of California Press, 2005), *The Lure of Images* (London: Routledge, 2007), and *The Embodied Eye* (Berkeley: University of California Press, 2012). He delivered the 2012 Cadbury Lectures at the University of Birmingham, England, on the visual history of Catholicism and Protestantism since the sixteenth century. The resulting book, *The Forge of Vision: Image and Imagination in Modern Christianity*, will appear in 2015 with the University of California Press.

JILL PETERFESO (Ph.D., University of North Carolina at Chapel Hill) is an assistant professor of religious studies at Guilford College in Greensboro, North Carolina. She is currently writing a monograph titled "*Womanpriest: Transgression and Tradition in the Contemporary Roman Catholic Church*." In addition to her work on American Catholicism, she has published on gender and sexuality in the Church of Jesus Christ of Latter-day Saints. Her article "From Testimony to Seximony, from Script to Scripture: Revealing Mormon Women's Sexuality through the Mormon Vagina Monologues," won a 2011 Elisabeth Schüssler Fiorenza New Scholars Award; it was published in the *Journal of Feminist Studies in Religion* 27, no. 2 (2011): 31–49.

LESLIE WOODCOCK TENTLER (Ph.D., University of Michigan) is a professor in the History Department of the Catholic University of America in Washington, D.C. Her books include *Wage-Earning Women: Industrial Employment and Family Life in the United States, 1900–1930* (New York: Oxford University Press, 1979), *Seasons of Grace: A History of the Catholic Archdiocese of Detroit* (Detroit: Wayne State University Press, 1990), and *Catholics and Contraception: An American History* (Ithaca: Cornell University Press, 2004). She edited *The Church Confronts Modernity: Catholicism since 1950 in the United States, the Republic of Ireland, and Quebec* (Washington, D.C.: Catholic University of America Press, 2007).

LUCAS VAN ROMPAY (Ph.D., Catholic University of Louvain, Belgium) is a professor of Eastern Christianity in the Department of Religious Studies at Duke University, North Carolina. His main fields of research are Syriac Christian literature and the history of Syriac Christianity. His most recent books include *Eusèbe d'Émèse. Commentaire de la Genèse. Texte arménien de l'édition de Venise (1980), fragments grecs et syriaques, avec traductions* (Louvain: Peeters, 2011), which he coauthored with Françoise Petit and J. J. S. Weitenberg, and *Catalogue of the Syriac Manuscripts and Fragments in the Library of Deir al-Surian (Egypt)* (Louvain: Peeters, 2014), which he coauthored with Sebastian P. Brock. With Sebastian P. Brock, Aaron M. Butts, and George A. Kiraz he coedited the *Gorgias Encyclopedic Dictionary of the Syriac Heritage* (Piscataway, N.J.: Gorgias Press, 2011).

# Index